The Mixing Bowl
Second Helpings

Our Lady's Hospice *&* Care Services

This book is dedicated to the men and women, residents, patients, families, volunteers, and staff who make Our Lady's Hospice & Care Services such a special place.

First Published in Ireland in 2017 by
Our Lady's Hospice & Care Services
Harold's Cross
Dublin 6W
D6W RY72
info@olh.ie
www.olh.ie

The Mixing Bowl: Second Helpings
ISBN: 978-1-5272-1122-3

Compiled by: The Fundraising & Communications Team @ Our Lady's Hospice & Care Services
Editing and project management by: Emma Walsh @ The Literary Professionals
Design, typeset and cover design by: Dave Darcy @ Dave Darcy Design
Illustrations by: Sarah Brownlee
Photography by: www.shutterstock.com

Photo of Neven Maguire's Chicken Thighs Braised in Cider with Sweet Potatoes
kindly supplied by Neven Maguire @ The MacNean Restaurant

Printed and bound in the United Kingdom by Fretwell Print & Design Ltd

Chapter Five: Desserts

Chapter Six: Cakes

Chapter Seven: Home Baking

Introduction

by Neven Maguire

A NEW COOK BOOK FROM OUR LADY'S HOSPICE IS SOMETHING TO CELEBRATE.

Some years back I was honoured to be asked to write a few words to go with a wonderful book of recipes that was contributed by clients of the Community Reablement Unit at Our Lady's Hospice & Care Services in Harold's Cross. I remember thinking at the time that the recipes brought me back so many memories of meals with families and friends over the years. Everyone has a few favourite recipes and I think they are all connected to memories, not of one meal, but of many meals at an earlier time of life.

Since I wrote that, I have seen the massive changes in what we, the Maguires, eat at home. The arrival of the twins has made Amelda and I think carefully about what they eat. We want them to get into the habit of using good local ingredients and knowing exactly what they are eating. There are plenty of ideas in this book that I am sure they will try before too long. I have no idea if either of them will ever want to be chefs. That is up to them and a long way away. But I do want them to respect the food they eat.

What we eat as a nation too is changing fast. We are so lucky to have great produce and that is the beginning of all good cooking. If I could change one thing I would like to see more people cooking at home. I would also like to see more young people cooking and being taught to cook the basics whether at home or in school or preferably both! It really is an important thing to be able to do.

But food is only part of the meal. The memories and feelings, conversations and fun that accompany our favourite recipes is a testament to the friends and family we have enjoyed them with. Amelda and I have made sure to keep time for us all to eat together without television and phones and all of the distractions. Surprisingly there has been little objection from the younger generation!

To respect and understand how to prepare the food we eat is good for our health. It is also good for family and friendships. Eating together is one of life's great pleasures. There are many great recipes in this book to try. If people mix new recipes with the ones they know well it is surprising how soon you build up a large repertoire of meals. This might sound odd coming from a restaurateur but no one can eat out all of the time! And I do have a cookery school in Blacklion where people are always welcome!

I hope you like my recipe for *Chicken Thighs Braised in Cider with Sweet Potatoes*. This recipe has to be one of my all-time favourites that I find myself returning to again and again. I look forward to introducing my family to some of the recipes in this book over the next while and I would like to compliment all of the contributors for the splendid recipes contained in this book.

Thank you again for asking me to add a few words to this lovely book. There is something in here for everyone. And remember, try some ones that are new to you, stretch those culinary muscles and you will not regret it.
I wish you all Happy Cooking,

Neven

Foreword

Following on from the first **Mixing Bowl** Cookbook, we pause for reflection on this new collection of stories and recipes so generously and smilingly offered to us from the residents, patients and their families of the Extended Care Unit (ECU), the Community Reablement Unit (CRU), the Rheumatic and Musculoskeletal Disease Unit (RMDU), together with wonderful Staff and Volunteers of Our Lady's Hospice & Care Services.

All the recipes have been tested, tasted, and rapturously enjoyed. Respecting the nuances and subtleties of each list of ingredients has been our first priority, so that our reader, who decides to make *Hollie and Katie's Flapjacks*, say, has no need to round up 250 g oats. For Patricia Betts' *Boatman's Pie*, you don't have to cook on a coal fire on the barge, but you will need an iron frying pan if you want the exact flavour.

But food is such an important part of the experience of life that the two are inextricably interwoven. Rhoda Nolan's philosophy of food emphasizes quality, and Betty Kennedy agrees, 'Use only the real thing!' Sylvia Doyle's philosophy simply says, 'I don't do negative,' and Susan Huszar's life experience is shared in her motto, 'a good temper, a sense of humour, and seeing the funny side of life turns reversals of fortune and disappointments into sunshine.' Alice Victory cautions us with this advice, 'Unless you want a new kitchen do not leave a can of condensed milk on the stove,' and if the cherries sink to the bottom of your cake, call it *Upside Down Delight*. Grace Murray, who lived five miles from anywhere, discovered that on Sundays, friends would increase their visits, often with an exclamation of 'Oh, I was just passing' on the off-chance that some scrumptious leftovers from dessert might be 'going-a-begging.'

So, if the *Mixing Bowl* appears to be a guidebook for the preparation of cakes and bakes, that is the case, but also, it is a sorcerer's anthology whose purpose is to create hope, imagination, conviviality, and happiness through breakfast, lunch, tea and dinner as lived and experienced by our contributors.

There is a magic quality within a recipe which, if you are lucky, transforms a list of ingredients into soul food. The memories of great food are the very memories of our lives. It is no surprise that Paul Reid chose to be eight years old in his story, remembering the love tucked inside his mother's chicken and bacon casserole. The mystery of a recipe, which we consider to be practically sacramental, lies of course in the love, comfort, sustenance, and conversation generated around this table, which you are now joining.

The secret happiness lies in this 'second giving', similar to handing a friend a cutting from your favourite rose or fruit tree. When a special recipe is transferred by way of a gift, an invitation, or a cookbook, to someone else, the magic increases. This is what happens in *The Mixing Bowl: Second Helpings*. It offers you, the reader, the accumulation of memory, wisdom, and sheer practical know-how, for your delight and delectation.

Isabel Cotter & Rose Kevany

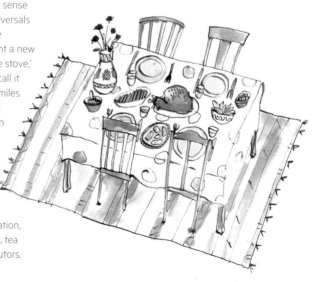

About Our Lady's Hospice & Care Services

"The care here is like a comfort blanket being wrapped around you… from the moment you enter, you know you're safe. And the comfort extends to family and friends whose worries are eased by knowing that their loved ones are so well cared for."
— *Palliative Care Patient*

Established in 1879, Our Lady's Hospice & Care Services is a 218 bed facility providing specialist and loving care for those with a wide range of needs from rehabilitation to end-of-life care.

This person-centred care is provided on-site in Harold's Cross and Blackrock Hospice as well as in people's own homes across south Dublin.

Our core values of human dignity, compassion, justice, quality and advocacy are at the heart of everything we do. While our ethos remains unaltered, the population we serve has changed radically. With the numbers of people aged over 65 set to almost triple in the next 30 years, we need to provide even more specialist facilities and services to ensure the highest quality of life for our patients and their families.

Just over 600 staff, 300 volunteers and one therapy dog work with patients and their families during difficult times. Their commitment is exceptional. We are especially grateful to our wonderful volunteers, without whom we would not be able to deliver the level of service that we do. We understand that each person has unique needs, and we treat our patients like family and the hospice as their home. We help patients live with comfort, dignity and peace of mind, treating the person and not the condition.

Specialist palliative care: palliative care is provided on both sites and through our 25 specialist community palliative care nurses, who provide over 12,300 homecare visits per year.

Long term care: Anna Gaynor House is our long-stay facility in Harold's Cross. Our residents include older people with chronic illness as well as younger residents with neurological conditions.

Community Reablement Unit: Based in Harold's Cross, our community reablement team works with over 65s who visit for rehabilitation support, which enables them to remain living independently in their own homes.

Rheumatic and Musculoskeletal Disease Unit: Our consultant-led team in Harold's Cross brings together experts from a range of disciplines to treat, support and care for those living with arthritis, rheumatic disease, fibromyalgia and other bone and muscle diseases. The goal is to empower patients and improve or maintain their quality of life.

During 2016, we cared for over 3,940 patients and residents, reflecting a 9% increase in patient numbers from 2015. Our teams undertook over 12,300 specialist palliative homecare visits, a 48% increase in demand since 2010.

We are currently undertaking the most ambitious project in our history: to bring our specialist palliative care services to even more people's homes and to develop 36 modern single palliative care rooms in Harold's Cross to ensure privacy, dignity and professional excellence at end-of-life.

Acknowledgements

We would like to give a very special thank you to the following people who made this book possible:

Dr SHEELA PERUMAL: who pioneered and guided the first book and whose idea it was to do it all again. We wish her and her family well in New Zealand and hope she approves of *The Mixing Bowl, Second Helpings*.

OCCUPATIONAL THERAPISTS CLAIRE O' BRIEN AND GERALDINE CONNOLLY who helped to establish this edition and who then handed the task to SINEAD MCGIRR AND AOIFE MCCORMACK without whose inspiration and cheerfulness we couldn't have managed.

VOLUNTEERS ROSE KEVANY AND ISABEL COTTER whose engagement with the patients in listening to and writing their stories is central to the character and atmosphere of the book.

VOLUNTEER CEPTA LYONS who kindly, enthusiastically and generously coordinated this project on behalf of the Hospice and Fundraising Team. Thank you, Cepta, you've created something wonderful here.

VOLUNTEER KATE LYONS who checked and tasted the recipes and shared her culinary expertise so generously.

We greatly appreciate the support of ARTIZAN FOOD COMPANY in sponsoring and providing the delightful catering for the book launch.

PHIL O'KELLY, Senior Fundraising Manager, who oversaw this project from concept to completion.

To our patient and understanding professionals: EMMA WALSH at The LITERARY PROFESSIONALS, Editor and Project Manager; DAVE DARCY, Graphic Designer; SARAH BROWNLEE, Illustrator, we owe a special thanks for all their invaluable guidance and support.

Finally thank you to all the patients, families, staff and volunteers wh
supported us throughout the planning and preparation of the book.

'Ar scáth a chéile a mhaireann na daoine.'

Eleanor Flew
Director of Fundraising & Communications.

Published by The Fundraising Department of
Our Lady's Hospital & Care Services

Chapter 1

Starters & Sides

Seafood Chowder
By Kate Lyons

This chowder was - until now – a top secret recipe of Kate's. Her parents were lucky enough to benefit from her willingness to cook and deliver it. Now that it's revealed, everyone else should try the recipe.

Preparation time 15 minutes *Cooking time* 45 minutes *Equipment* Large saucepan *Serves* 6

Ingredients

120g/4½oz butter
2 white onions, finely diced
4 cloves garlic, crushed
120g/4½oz plain flour
3 vegetable stock cubes (or fish)
1½ litres/2½ pints water

300g/10½oz carrots, peeled and diced
300g/10½oz potatoes, peeled and diced
250ml/8½fl oz cream

400g/14oz mixed fish, including 100g smoked fish, in chunky pieces
150g/5oz cooked prawns
2 tablespoons flat leafed parsley

Method

1. In a pot over a medium heat, melt the butter and add the onion and garlic.

2. Cook for 3-5 minutes until translucent.

3. Add the flour and stock cubes, stirring all the time. It should look like sand.

4. Cook out the flour for approximately 4 minutes, making sure it does not stick.

5. Add the water, a small amount at a time, stirring well between each addition.

6. Add the cream. Stir the pot every few minutes to make sure the flour does not fall to the bottom and burn.

7. Bring to the boil then reduce the heat and add the diced carrots and potatoes.

8. Cook for 20 minutes, approximately, depending on the size of the carrots and potatoes.

9. When the vegetables are just cooked, add the diced fish and cook for a further 5 minutes until the fish is just cooked.

10. Add the prawns. These should only take a few minutes to heat through.

11. Stir in the parsley and serve with brown soda bread or crusty white French bread.

Canadian Pâté

By Barbara Mainey

Pâté is surprisingly easy to make at home. This version adds Worcestershire sauce for an extra kick.

Preparation time 10 minutes *Cooking time* 60-70 minutes
Equipment 1lb loaf tin, lined with parchment paper *Serves* 8-10

Ingredients

1 tablespoon vegetable oil
1 large onion, finely chopped
4 cloves garlic, finely chopped
250g/½lb rashers, diced
450g/1lb lamb or chicken liver
1 bay leaf

1 teaspoon Worcestershire sauce
Salt and pepper
100ml/3 tablespoons stock
100ml/3 tablespoons sherry or red wine

Method

1. Place the oil in a frying pan and fry the onion, garlic and rashers gently for 5 minutes.

2. Add all the remaining ingredients and simmer for 30-35 minutes.

3. Allow to cool slightly then remove the bay leaf.

4. Preheat the oven to 180C/350F/Gas mark 4.

5. Liquidise the mixture until smooth and season to taste.

6. Place the mixture in the prepared loaf tin and place in the oven.

7. Bake for 30-35 minutes. When completely cooled, remove from the tin and store in the fridge. The pâté will keep for 4-5 days.

Barbara was the eldest of six children and learned to think 'the hard way' as a result of growing up during World War II. Life under the sirens was tough and a consistent education impractical. When she was 11 years-old her father told her, 'don't even bother, you will not be going to school.' She went out to work at 14 and never looked back. She made sure she set education as a priority for her own daughter, teaching her how to think and how to learn.

Barbara sews, knits, gardens, paints. She makes miniature soft furnishings for dolls houses: blankets, curtains, cushions, and carpets, all in pretty flowery colours, to match the wallpaper. Her hands are less flexible now, due to arthritis and she says, 'When you used to do something and you can't do it, you want to forget.'

She is philosophical, however, about her own journey and the unexpected paths life takes, 'life has chosen me,' she says, 'you become a product of your life, and at the end of your life, you are not necessarily what you planned to be, but you survive, in fact, you can thrive.'

Stir-Fried Cabbage

By Eilish Byrne

This is delicious on its own or served with bacon and mash.

Eilish worked in the *Well Fed Café* in Temple Bar in 1987, when vegetarian cooking was considered too difficult to cook or eat. The café specialized in tasty, innovative and original dishes, and became so popular that there were queues outside the door at lunchtime. They joke that they saved Temple Bar!

Preparation time 15 minutes *Cooking time* 10 minutes
Equipment Frying pan or wok *Serves* 4

Ingredients

1 head cabbage, savoy/green
2 onions, finely chopped
6 cloves garlic, crushed
8 medium mushrooms, thinly sliced

1 teaspoon ground cumin
Pinch of cayenne pepper
Pinch of salt
1 teaspoon lemon juice
Oil for frying

Method

1. Cut the cabbage lengthwise into long, thin strips.

2. Heat the pan and put in a tablespoon of oil. Heat until smoking slightly.

3. Fry the mushrooms, onions and garlic until soft, then add the cumin.

4. Add the cabbage a handful at a time, and cook for 3-4 minutes until the cabbage is tender.

5. Add the cayenne pepper, salt and lemon juice, and stir well.

6. Serve immediately and enjoy.

Garlic Roast Potato Wedges
By Adrienne Parkes

This recipe was given to Adrienne many years ago by a Canadian friend.

Preparation time 10 minutes *Cooking time* 10-15 minutes *Equipment* Large baking tray *Serves* 4-6

Ingredients

4 large potatoes,
  roosters are good
50g/2oz butter

4 tablespoons parmesan
  cheese, grated

1 teaspoon garlic, crushed
½ teaspoon salt and pepper

Method

1. Preheat the oven to 220C/425F/Gas mark 7.

2. Cut the potatoes into wedges and boil until quite tender.

3. In a large saucepan, melt the butter.

4. Then stir in the cheese, garlic, and salt and pepper.

5. Pour the potatoes into the saucepan and coat them with the butter mixture.

6. Spread onto a baking tray and bake in the preheated oven for 10-15 minutes.

Marmalade

By Clemency Emmet

This is a really accessible recipe for making marmalade, something so many people are afraid to try at home. Try it and you'll love it!

Preparation time 45 minutes, plus overnight
Cooking time Up to 90 minutes *Equipment* Jam jars *Makes* 8 jars

Ingredients

1½kg/3lbs large Valencia or Seville oranges

3 small lemons

2½litres/5 pints water

3kg/6lbs granulated sugar, warmed*

Method

1. Scrub the fruit well, cut into quarters and remove the pips and pith.

2. Soak the oranges in the water for 24 hours.

3. The next day, boil the mixture for 1 hour in the water it has been soaking in.

4. Add the warmed sugar*.

5. Continue to boil the marmalade for another 10 minutes until a jelly forms.

6. To test the jelly: scoop up a small amount of jelly in a spoon, cool it slightly and let it drop back into the pan from the side of the spoon. As the syrup thickens, two large drops will form on the either edge of the spoon. When these drops come together, or coalesce, into a single drop, this is the 'sheeting stage', when the jelly reaches 220C.

7. Cooking time required for this stage ranges from 8 to 30 minutes.

8. Store in sterilized** jars to help the jam last.

*To warm sugar: spread on a tray in the oven at 150C/300F/Gas mark 2 for 10-15 minutes.
**To sterilize jars: half-fill jars with cold water and place in the microwave on high heat until the water is bubbling. Empty jars and store upside-down on a clean cloth until required.

January

In the slow domestic rhythm of the year
January was the month of marmalade
It came as a cleansing ritual,
the careful shredding of bitter oranges,
the sliding of sugar into the boiling pan.
Its golden heart lighting the winter day.
We filled the line of brilliant jars
as if, briefly, we could bottle the sun.

'January' by Clemency Emmet, from her poetry collection 'Fire Seed'.

Parsley Lemonade Liquor
By Clemency Emmet

This refreshing twist to a lemonade recipe will transport you back to old country ways.

Preparation time 20 minutes
Cooking time 10 minutes plus chilling time
Equipment Large saucepan *Makes* Approximately 5 pints

Ingredients

8 lemons, juice and rind
200g/7oz white sugar
500ml/¾ pint water

Several sprigs of fresh parsley, chopped finely
Grated lemon rind to serve

Method

1. First make the syrup by boiling the water and sugar together for 5 minutes.

2. Cut or peel the rind of the lemons into strips and add to the water and sugar mixture.

3. Chill the mixture.

4. Add the juice of the lemons and stir well.

5. Strain the liquid to remove the lemon rind and chill again.

6. This syrup can be stored in a covered jar in the fridge and used as needed.

7. To make up the lemonade add 2 tablespoons of the syrup to 250ml/½ pint water.

8. Add one teaspoon of chopped parsley.

9. Stir well and serve with a sprinkling of grated lemon rind.

Holiday With Norah

We knew every turn in the road that led
to your white farmhouse at the lake's edge.
You would be standing at the open door,
your welcome as warm as the glowing turf fire.

To us children, your house was magic;
We slept in two brass beds, set end to end,
the windows, wide open to the sweet air
brought in the twilight rustling hens.
'I hung a lantern for you', you said,
and we looked out together at the moon
sailing high over the still lake.

Every day we feasted at the kitchen table
Bacon, cut from the side, hung in smoky rafters.
Eggs, new laid, brown bread from the turf oven,
your own butter, apple tarts and cream.
We did not think of those cold early mornings
when you milked the Kerry cow who kicked
- the milky cross you drew on her side
was a prayer for safety and thanksgiving –
you would separate the thick cream,
and work the churn, over and under, till butter came.
Every drop of water you carried from the well,
Icy-cold, iron-tasting, in heavy silver buckets.
The every day and every week of labour
Was poured out for us in shining plenty.

And we, happy, loved, replete,
Believed you lived in paradise.

'Norah', by Clemency Emmet,
from her poetry collection, 'Fire Seed'.

Kate's Dip
By Noreen Buckley

This is a cherished recipe from Noreen's granddaughter, Kate, and is so simple and quick to make.

Preparation time 5 minutes *Cooking time* 0 minutes
Equipment Small serving dish *Serves* 6-8 with vegetables to dip

Ingredients

250g/8oz fat-free
cottage cheese
1 tablespoon lemon juice

2 tablespoons skimmed milk
½ packet onion soup mix

Method

1. Mix together the cottage cheese and lemon juice in a blender.

2. Add the skimmed milk and soup mix and blend again.

3. Chill before serving with fresh vegetables, such as carrots, celery and peppers.

Noreen grew up in her grandparents' house from the age of three. She recalls it explained to her she was 'given away as a present' as she was part of a large family. Six more siblings were born after and she always asked 'why me?' Unsurprisingly, she resented the loss of her family and the hurt became part of the person she grew to be.

At sixteen, independent and self-sufficient, she moved to live with her uncle in New York. In 1956, a leap year, aged 21, Noreen's cousin gave her a raffle ticket for a dance she could not attend.

At the dance Noreen pulled a ticket from the raffle and won. Looking around she asked 'what have I won?' and was told 'you can choose any man you like for your husband.' She looked out and noticed William Buckley. They were married two years later and returned home to Ireland together with their three children.

Noreen has to use a walker now to get around but is positive and determined. She has a recipe of her own for getting through the bad days: 'I stop thinking about things for a while. Have a good cry; it helps. Keep busy. Put my hands into flour, or earth. Bake. Garden. I keep up hope and pray that tomorrow will be better than today.'

Chapter 2

Light Bites

Party Pizza
By Betty Kennedy

Great for adults' and children's parties alike.

Preparation time 35 minutes *Cooking time* 18-20 minutes
Equipment 25 x 15cm/10 x 6 inch Swiss roll tin, greased *Serves* 4-6

Ingredients

Base:
225g/8oz self-raising flour
100g/4oz butter
Water to mix
(ready-made pastry also works very well)
Topping:
225g/8oz sausage meat
1 large onion, finely chopped

4 large eggs, beaten
Salt and pepper to taste
225g/8oz tomatoes, finely chopped
150g/6oz mushrooms, sliced
225g/8oz ham, cut into pieces
50g/2oz cheddar cheese, grated
Black olives for decoration

Method

1. Preheat the oven to 180C/350F/Gas mark 4.
2. Make the pizza base first by rubbing the flour and butter together with the tips of your fingers until the mixture resembles fine breadcrumbs.
3. Add enough water to make a soft pastry.
4. Roll out to the size of the tin and lay it on top of the greased tin. Set aside and reserve any leftover pieces for later.
5. Next start preparing the toppings.
6. Break up the sausage meat and fry until cooked, then set aside.
7. Fry the onion in the same pan until the onion becomes soft and transparent.
8. Spread the onion and sausage meat on the pizza base.
9. Beat the eggs and add some salt and pepper. Pour this over the onion and sausage meat on the pizza base.
10. Place the tomatoes, mushrooms and ham on top.
11. Sprinkle grated cheddar over the entire pizza.
12. Roll out the leftover pastry very thinly and cut into narrow strips the length of the pizza base.
13. Place the strips in a trellis pattern on top of the pizza.
14. Place half a black olive at each intersection of trellis.
15. Bake in the preheated oven for 18-20 minutes.
16. Cut into squares or fingers to serve.

Betty's mother worked as a maid in a 'big house' in England. As Betty describes her: 'she was the sort of person who made macaroni and cheese if there were no potatoes. Nothing flustered her.' She was a wise and inspiring woman and her fortitude is a character trait shared by Betty.

One of nine of children, Betty worked in a grocery store on Parnell Street, and then in a hair salon on Wicklow Street. What did she learn from both experiences? A simple but useful life lesson... 'How to make life more pleasant? A nice cup of tea!' Betty met her husband when she was 21 and they lived happily ever after for the next sixty years. Sadly he died two years ago, aged 93. She is blessed with five children, and seventeen grandchildren.

Putting her attitude to life and its challenges into words Betty offers this:
'In this Valley of Tears, you need to allow yourself to feel – it's ok to feel emotion, so do not shy away from it. You can go with your emotions, it is quite normal to feel them but the secret lies in your decision to prepare yourself so you can come to terms with reality.'

She humorously follows this up with wise words from another wise woman... 'As Mrs. Brown says, "Try not to die 'til Friday."'

Buckwheat Galettes

By Margot Kenny

Margot acquired this recipe while travelling in France and it is still a very important part of her cooking repertoire. These crepes can be made in advance, then filled and baked when required.

Preparation time 10 minutes, plus 2 hours in fridge *Cooking time* 25 minutes
Equipment 20cm/8 inch crepe or frying pan *Serves* 3

Ingredients

Batter:
160g/6oz buckwheat flour
45g/1½oz roasted buckwheat groats, finely ground (optional, available in most supermarkets and health-food stores)

65g/2oz plain flour
2 large eggs
600ml/1 pint buttermilk
½ teaspoon salt, plus extra if needed

Filling:
2 tablespoons butter, melted
180g/6½oz asparagus, trimmed and peeled
6 slices cooked ham
200g/7oz gruyère cheese, grated

Method

1. Make the batter by whisking together both flours, the groats, eggs, buttermilk, and salt until well combined.

2. Leave the batter in the fridge for at least 2 hours or preferably overnight.

3. When ready to cook, preheat the oven to 200C/400F/Gas mark 6.

4. Heat a pan over a medium/high heat.

5. Rub a little butter on the pan and pour about 100ml of the batter in.

6. Swirl the pan to spread the batter evenly.

7. Cook for about 1 minute then flip carefully with a spatula.

8. Cook for a further 1 minute on the other side.

9. Set aside and continue to make the rest, stacking them as they are cooked.

10. Cook the asparagus in boiling, salted water for 2 minutes and drain on kitchen paper.

11. To fill the crepes: lay each one top-side down, place a slice of ham on top, sprinkle generously with grated cheese, then lay 3 asparagus spears on top to the side. Fold over to make a half-moon shape.

12. Place the crepes on a baking sheet, drizzle with melted butter, and bake until they are crisp and the cheese is melted, about 5-7 minutes. Serve immediately.

Chinese Sweet Pork Chops

By Alex Carroll

A simple Irish staple of pork chops is turned into an exotic meal with the addition of Chinese herbs and spices.

Preparation time 15 minutes *Cooking time* 60 minutes
Equipment Large Pan with lid *Serves* 4

Ingredients

4 pork chops,
cut into small cubes
1 star anise
1 inch cinnamon stick
1 bay leaf
Thumb-sized piece of root
ginger, grated
2 garlic cloves, crushed

2 medium leeks, sliced
1 tablespoons balsamic vinegar
1 tablespoon water
2 tablespoons each of soya
sauce, brown sugar, dry sherry
4 spring onions, sliced
1 tablespoon lemon juice

Method

1. Heat a large frying pan until slightly smoking and put in a splash of oil.

2. Add the pork and cook to seal the meat. Remove from the pan and set aside.

3. Lower the heat and add the star anise, cinnamon, bay leaf, ginger and garlic.

4. Cook for 2 minutes.

5. Add the leeks and cook until softened.

6. Put the pork back into the pan and add the balsamic vinegar, water, soya sauce, brown sugar and dry sherry and bring to the boil.

7. Reduce the heat, cover, and simmer for one hour.

8. Season with salt and pepper and add a tablespoon of lemon juice.

9. Garnish with chopped spring onions and serve with rice.

Alex lived in Australia but decided to make Ireland his permanent home. He is a massive foodie and a cookery show addict. He takes the recipes he sees and substitutes, refines, and changes elements as he goes along. His mother instilled a love of cooking in him from a young age and it was nurtured along by his aunt, who was a professional chef at The Clarence Hotel. He looks for dishes from all corners of the earth; he has travelled to China to dine on Mao Tse Tung's favourite dish, Hunanese Red-Braised Pork, with different ingredients from his own recipe: Shaoxing wine, red chillies, cinnamon sticks, cassia bark... but actually, he found it rather disappointing!

Between tasting and travelling he likes to walk in Phoenix Park with his boxer, Lewis (named after Lennox), enjoys a glass of beer in the sunshine, and is a fishing addict in all weathers. He loves reading and his favourite author is Georges Simenon, creator of the fictional detective Maigret. Alex has a PhD in Clinical Psychology and works with teenagers, using drama and role-playing often as experiments and to help them process all sorts of experiences and rehearse how they will manage their futures. Alongside these great passions; food, literature, psychology, Alex's other great joy is to organize street parties to raise funds for the Hospice.

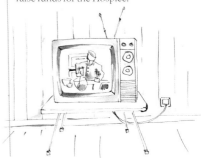

Gluten-Free Salmon and Broccoli Quiche

Rita Gallagher

This is just one of many recipes which can easily be adapted to suit different food allergies by replacing some of the ingredients with an alternative version.

Preparation time 20 minutes *Cooking time* 30 minutes
Equipment 20cm/8 inch flan tin, greased; and parchment paper *Serves* 6-8

Ingredients

1 large onion, finely chopped
110g/4oz mushrooms
225g/8oz broccoli, fresh or frozen
180g/6oz gluten-free flour
¼ teaspoon salt

½ teaspoon black pepper
55g/2oz oat bran
85g/3oz butter
6 large eggs, beaten
580ml/1 pint milk or soya milk

110g/4oz cheddar cheese, grated
110g/4oz cooked or tinned salmon
1 tablespoon dill

Method

1. Preheat the oven to 180C/350F/Gas mark 4.

2. Place the onions and mushrooms in the microwave on high for two minutes, or fry for 4 minutes.

3. If using fresh broccoli, cook for 5 minutes in boiling water.

4. Sieve the flour, salt and pepper into a large bowl. Add the bran.

5. Rub butter into the mixture until it resembles fine breadcrumbs.

6. Add the eggs, milk, and half the cheese to the dry ingredients and mix well.

7. Fold in the broccoli, salmon, onions and mushrooms.

8. Season and add the dill.

9. Pour the mixture into the quiche tin and sprinkle the remaining cheese on top.

10. Bake in the preheated oven for 30 minutes, or until the quiche is well-risen and golden on top.

Salmon Cheese Roll
By Diarmaid Morton

Diarmaid has given this recipe (that his wife, Nuala, prepares!) as one of his favourites. The recipe originated in Canada and has passed on to friends and family who, having tasted the dish, desperately needed the recipe!

Preparation time **10 minutes** *Chilling time:* **several hours or overnight**
Equipment **Shallow serving plate** *Serves* **6-8**

Ingredients

225g/8oz cream cheese (full fat)
225g/8oz cooked fresh salmon
1 tablespoon lemon juice
1 teaspoon minced onion

1 teaspoon creamed horseradish
Salt and pepper to taste

To garnish:
2 tablespoons chopped fresh parsley
100g pecans, chopped

Method

1. Remove the skin and bones from the salmon then flake into pieces.

2. Combine the salmon and all other ingredients and mix well.

3. Chill for several hours or overnight.

4. Combine the parsley and pecans and place in a separate shallow dish.

5. Shape the mixture into a roll and then roll in the parsley and pecans to cover it.

6. Refrigerate until required. It can be made up to two days in advance.

7. Cut the roll into slices and serve with a salad or crackers or both.

Red Cabbage and Pomegranate Salad
By Mary Cunningham

Mary loves this recipe. It is so refreshing and goes beautifully with roast lamb.

Preparation time 10 minutes *Cooking time* 10 minutes *Equipment* Bowl for serving *Serves* 6-8

Ingredients

1 red cabbage, sliced or grated
Salt and black pepper

2 tablespoons olive oil
Juice of 1 lemon
2 pomegranates

1 red onion, finely sliced
Large bunch mint leaves, chopped

Method

1. Slice or grate the cabbage in a food processor and season well with salt and pepper.
2. Leave for at least 10 minutes.
3. Mix the oil and lemon juice together and stir into the cabbage
4. To remove the seeds from the pomegranate, cut it in half and strike it with a wooden spoon; the seeds will just fall out.
5. Add the seeds, the onion and the mint to the cabbage mixture and mix. Keep refrigerated until required.

Salmon & Leek Flan w/ Dill & Crème Fraîche

By Eleanor Flew

Eleanor offers us this recipe, which she has 'borrowed' from her mother-in-law, Denise Leahy in Wexford.

Preparation time 30 minutes *Cooking time* 45-50 minutes
Equipment 20cm/8 inch flan tin, greased *Serves* 4

Ingredients

Base:*
150g/6oz plain flour
80g/3oz butter
Pinch of salt
Cold water to bind

Filling:
225g/8oz salmon fillets
200ml/7fl oz water
1 fish stock cube
1 leek, sliced

250g/8oz crème fraîche
Few sprigs of dill
Salt and pepper to taste
*ready-made shortcrust pastry also works well

Method

1. Preheat the oven to 180C/350F/Gas mark 4.
2. Rub the flour and butter together using the tips of your fingers, until the mixture resembles fine breadcrumbs.
3. Add enough water to bind to a stiff dough.
4. Roll out onto a board to the size of the tin, then line the tin with the pastry, pressing firmly into the sides, trim the edges.
5. Cover the pastry with parchment paper, place a layer of baking beans (or any dried pulse) on top and bake in the preheated oven for 15 minutes.
6. Remove the beans and bake for a further 5 minutes. Set aside and make the filing.
7. Poach the salmon fillets in fish stock made from the stoccube and 200ml boiling water, then drain and retain 2 tablespoons of the stock. Allow the salmon to cool, then flake into large pieces.
8. Fry the leek until just tender.
9. Mix half of the crème fraîche with the 2 tablespoons of the stock, then add the rest of the crème fraîche, and lightly fold in the salmon and the leek.
10. Add the chopped dill and season to taste. Pour the mixture into the flan case and bake for 30-35 minutes.
11. Garnish with a few sprigs of dill. Serve hot or cold with stuffed tomatoes and a salad.

Chapter 3

Main Meals
Meat & Poultry

Boatman's Stew

By Patricia Betts

This simple stew is so quick and easy to make, just 30 minutes from start to finish!

Preparation time **10 minutes** *Cooking time* **15-20 minutes**
Equipment **Large frying pan** *Serves* **4-6**

Ingredients

8 rashers of bacon, fat included
3 medium onions, chopped

6 large potatoes, peeled and cut into thin slices
Pepper and salt to taste

Method

1. Fry the rashers on both sides and set aside.

2. Fry the onions in the bacon fat until they are transparent and well cooked. Add a little extra oil, if required.

3. Lay the rashers on the base of the pan, cover them with the onions then seal the pan with the potato slices.

4. Season with pepper and salt.

5. Fill the pan with water up to the level of the potatoes.

6. Cook over a coal, gas, electric, or camping stove until the potatoes are cooked, approximately 15 minutes.

This recipe was named by Patricia in honour of her father, Patrick, who created it while working as 'Master' on a coal barge on the Royal Canal. He was much-loved for his genius in not only developing this tasty stew but also for frequently bringing along the ingredients to work with him to cook it for his mates. He used to prepare the iron frying pan with a little oil and gently shake it while it lay on the coal fire in the cabin to keep the stew from sticking. This dish gave Patricia's father a sense of pride and joy, the feeling a chef gets when they prepare a meal for family and friends. Patricia remembers how he always made those around him feel so special.

Patrick was born in the 1920s, a time when most boys did not benefit from the education they deserved. These constraints, however, did nothing to stop him learning. His voracious appetite for information, much like his appetite for food, extended far and wide. He read Lenin and Marx for pleasure and was intrigued by the political paradox of the working man; how he could enact change through casting his vote, yet still remain economically disadvantaged.

Outside of work and education, his other passions were his family and the outdoors. He was a keen runner and combined these interests by running regularly with Patricia in the Phoenix Park, well into his seventies. His one simple rule for his family was, 'keep in touch, get together, and remember all occasions' and that was his own recipe for keeping his family close. He was much-loved.

Moroccan Lamb

By Sylvia Doyle

This is a great recipe for entertaining. Place in the oven three hours before your guests arrive, then relax!

Preparation time 15 mins plus overnight in the fridge
Cooking time 3 hours
Equipment Large casserole dish with lid *Serves* 6-8

Ingredients

1.3kg/3lbs diced lamb
1 large onion, finely chopped
4 cloves garlic, chopped
1 tablespoon fresh ginger, grated
Grated rind of 1 lemon
1 tablespoon ground cumin
1 tablespoon ground coriander
2 teaspoons cayenne pepper
1 teaspoon ground black pepper

1 teaspoon paprika
1 teaspoon turmeric
10 dried prunes, quartered
2 tins chopped tomatoes
300ml/½ pint good chicken stock
To Serve:
100g/3oz couscous per person
250g/8oz Greek yogurt
4 tablespoons olive oil
Grated zest of lemon or lime

Method

1. Place all ingredients, except the olive oil, into the casserole dish.

2. Mix well, cover and leave in the fridge overnight.

3. Next day, about 3 hours before required, preheat the oven to 150C/300F/Gas mark 2.

4. Put the casserole in the oven and cook for approximately 3 hours.

5. Cook the couscous according to the manufacturer's instructions.

6. When cooked, drizzle olive oil over the casserole.

7. Serve on a large platter with a dish of Greek yogurt mixed with grated lemon or lime.

The Hospice has had a very special role in Sylvia's life. The Community Palliative Care Team supported Sylvia and her sister Betty in caring for their mother when she became terminally ill.

Sylvia says they were blessed to have the support from the team. They looked after her, monitored her, and kept her pain-free. Along with all the practical help from the team, their friends Evangeline and Chris set up a system of visitors, so her mother was always kept company and never felt isolated.

'I never encountered so much love as in this place,' says Sylvia.

Chicken Chorizo Hotpot

By Bernadette Pirihi

Chorizo, a spicy Spanish pork sausage, is full of flavour and makes this a hotpot bursting with taste and colour. Try serving it with crusty bread, rice, and salad.

Preparation time 15 minutes *Cooking time* 1 hour 10 minutes
Equipment Large frying pan *Serves* 4

Ingredients

12cm/5 inch chorizo sausage
4 chicken breasts, cut into thick strips
400g tin chopped tomatoes

2 chicken stock cubes
1 teaspoon sweet paprika
2 tablespoons Worcestershire sauce

1 tin chickpeas, drained
Salt and pepper to taste

Method

1. Slice the chorizo into thin slices and fry on the pan for 3 minutes, no oil required. Set aside.

2. Cook the chicken in the oil from the chorizo for 5 minutes.

3. Place the chorizo, chicken, tomatoes, stock cubes, sweet paprika and Worcestershire sauce into the pan.

4. Bring to the boil, then cook on a low heat for 60 minutes.

5. Add the chickpeas and simmer on low for a further 10 minutes.

6. Season with salt and pepper to taste.

Chicken Curry

By Desmond Gibney

A great accompaniment to this easy curry is a German Altbier (a German-style brown ale).

Preparation time 10 minutes *Cooking time* 45 minutes
Equipment Heavy-bottomed saucepan *Serves* 6/7

Ingredients

1 onion, finely chopped

2 tablespoons mild curry powder

2 cloves garlic, crushed

2 teaspoons ginger, finely grated

1 green or red chilli, deseeded and finely chopped, (optional)

1 tin of chopped tomatoes

1 teaspoon tomato purée

8 chicken breasts, diced

1 tin of coconut milk

½ jar of mango chutney

Lots of coriander

Salt and freshly ground black pepper

This recipe was submitted by Desmond in memory of his friend Eoin Fennessy (Fenno), who was cared for in Our Lady's Hospice & Care Services, Harold's Cross during August & September 2016. Eoin had a great sense of adventure; in travel and in food. He always enjoyed his food and especially loved experimenting with new dishes.

Eoin's illness didn't define him but perhaps the way he faced it did. He didn't beat his illness, but he certainly left behind many reasons for his friends to celebrate his life. As Fenno, himself, would say, 'onwards and upwards!'

Method

1. Cook the onions in the saucepan on a low heat in some oil until they become translucent.

2. Add the diced chicken and fry for 10 minutes.

3. Add the curry powder and cook for another minute.

4. Add everything else in one go and mix well.

5. Bring to the boil and simmer for about 45 minutes, until the chicken is cooked.

6. Serve with basmati, wholegrain or white rice; whatever you like best!

Sticky Mango Chicken
By Josephine Herlihy

Chicken is such a staple in so many people's diets but it can often be difficult to figure out how to liven it up, this clever recipe will do just that.

Preparation time 10 minutes plus 30 minutes to marinade *Cooking time* 11 minutes stir-frying or 30 minutes in the oven *Equipment* Wok or casserole dish *Serves* 6

Ingredients

6 chicken breasts
(cut into chunks)
1 ripe mango
(peeled and chopped)

For marinade
¼ teaspoon dried crushed chilies
2 garlic cloves, finely chopped
1 tablespoon grated fresh ginger
½ lime, zest and juice

3 tablespoons light muscovado sugar
1 tablespoon soy sauce
1 tablespoon olive oil
2 tablespoons mango chutney

Method

1. Combine all the marinade ingredients (except for the chutney) together and mix well.

2. Add the chicken and toss so all the pieces are well coated.

3. Marinate for 30 minutes or more.

4. Heat a wok over a high heat.

5. Add the marinated chicken and stir fry for 10 minutes, stirring frequently until sticky, charred and cooked through.

6. Add the mango and stir for a further 1 minute.

7. You can also bake the chicken in a casserole dish in a preheated oven 180C/350F/Gas mark 4.

8. Cook for 25 minutes then stir in the mango chutney and cook for another 3 to 4 minutes.

9. Serve hot with brown rice and a green salad.

Kebabs Robana Bhorat

By Lucy Carroll

This is a recipe Lucy received many years ago from a friend visiting from India. It quickly became a firm favourite among family and friends.

Preparation time 10 minutes plus 2 hours to marinade *Cooking time* 20 minutes
Equipment Frying pan and saucepan *Serves* 4-6

Ingredients

Meatballs
1kg/2lbs beef, minced very finely (ask your butcher to do this)
1½ teaspoons ground ginger
1½ teaspoons garlic powder
1 teaspoon red chilli powder
¼ teaspoon cinnamon powder
¼ teaspoon ground cloves
1 teaspoon ground coriander
½ teaspoon ground cumin
½ teaspoon turmeric
Oil or butter for frying
1 large onion, finely chopped

Sauce
1 tin of tomatoes
½ teaspoon red chilli powder
Salt and pepper to taste
Parsley or coriander leaves to garnish

Method

1. Make the meatballs first. Add all the spices to the mince and mix them through thoroughly.

2. Leave to marinate in the fridge for 2 hours.

3. Fry the onion in oil until golden and just crisp.

4. Drain it on kitchen paper and let it cool.

5. When cold and crisp, crush the onion into powder and add to the mince mixture.

6. Roll the mince into golf-ball-sized pieces and fry slowly for at least 20 minutes, turning at least once.

7. Next, liquidise all the ingredients for the sauce together.

8. Pour into a saucepan and simmer for 10 minutes.

9. Serve the meatballs on kebab sticks with the sauce drizzled over.

10. Garnish with fresh parsley or coriander leaves.

Microwave Chicken Curry

By Pauline Foy

A simple and easy to prepare dinner using leftover chicken; a joy to eat on a Wintry Monday!

Preparation time 5 minutes *Cooking time* 15 minutes
Equipment Microwave-proof dish and microwave *Serves* 2

Ingredients

1 medium onion, chopped

1 medium cooking apple, peeled and chopped

1 tablespoon sunflower oil

5 teaspoons curry powder (hot or medium according to taste)

1 tablespoon plain flour

1 heaped tablespoon mango chutney

400ml/14fl oz good chicken stock

200g/7oz cooked chicken

Chopped pineapple for garnish

Method

1. Put the onion, apple and oil into the microwave-proof dish with the lid on and heat for 4 minutes on a medium-high temperature in the microwave.

2. Add the curry powder, flour, chutney, and stock and mix through.

3. Heat for 4 more minutes, on a medium heat, stirring after 2 minutes.

4. Add the cooked chicken and heat through for a further 6-8 minutes, on a medium heat, stirring after 3 minutes.

5. Serve with boiled rice and garnish with chopped pineapple.

Although Pauline has contributed a main meal recipe, it was always baking that was in her blood.

One of seven children, she grew up helping her mother make endless apple tarts, bread and cakes. After school she trained at Dundrum Technical School where she made her first Christmas cake. It was such a hit that she recalls her neighbour, Mr. Fassbender, telling her to name her price when he saw it on the sideboard!

Her first job, aptly enough, was in Manning's Bakery, Thomas Street. She was quartermaster, meaning it was her job to decide which bakery items must be ordered for the next day. Later, as pastry chef, she would fill trays of baked shells with whipped cream to transform them into eclairs, and stripe them with chocolate sauce. She perfected her icing skills and would ice the cupcakes with hot pink, neon blue, and shocking green colours. Of course, staying trim in this type of job is never easy but, showing great discipline, she shed over three stone.

Working in the bakery was a great way to meet and chat to people. Everyone who came in greeted her and years later, she would continue to encounter people who would say: 'Sure I know you! I bought turnovers from you.'

Veal Valdostana

By Anna Gentile

This is Anna's favourite recipe from her own restaurant *Quo Vadis.*

Preparation time 10 minutes *Cooking time* 10 minutes
Equipment Non-stick pan and baking tray *Serves* 4

Ingredients

100g/3oz dried breadcrumbs
3 tablespoons of plain flour
Salt and pepper to taste
1 large egg beaten with 2
tablespoons of water
4 veal cutlets, rolled out thinly
12 sticks asparagus,
lightly steamed
125g/4ozs Fontina cheese

Butter for frying
8 lemon wedges for garnish

Tomato Sauce:
1 tin tomatoes
3 cloves garlic, crushed
1 carrot, grated
1 medium onion, chopped

Method

1. Preheat the oven to 180C/350F/Gas mark 6.

2. Spread the breadcrumbs on a large plate and set aside.

3. Combine the flour, salt and pepper in a bowl and dip the cutlets into the mixture, coating carefully.

4. Now dip each cutlet into the beaten egg mixture, then into the breadcrumbs, being careful to coat all over.

5. Heat the butter in a non-stick pan until hot and bubbly, then fry the cutlets on both sides, for about 3 minutes each side.

6. Transfer the cutlets to a baking tray and place three sticks of asparagus on each.

7. Top off each cutlet with 1oz of the cheese.

8. Heat under the grill until the cheese just melts.

9. Make the sauce by simmering the tomatoes, garlic, carrot and onion in a large saucepan for 20-30 minutes.

10. Serve each portion of veal with 2 lemon wedges and the tomato sauce.

Anna was born in Ireland but as her parents were Italian, she lived as an Italian here, eating only Italian food and eventually marrying her favourite Italian, Bernardino Gentile. Together they ran Quo Vadis restaurant on Wicklow Street for thirty-one years. 'We enjoyed a wonderful clientele; lots of newspaper reporters and so on. Everyone loved the menu and they kept coming back; we knew their preferences.'

Quo Vadis opened at 6pm, and was supposed to close at 1am, but often ran on much later than that. When the restaurant finally did close each night Anna and Bernardino would go on to other restaurants for a couple of starters because they knew all the other chefs in the restaurants around Dublin.

Anna freely admits that they could not have lived this sort of nocturnal life without the help of her mother, who helped them with their three children, or as Anna laughs; 'lived her life happily fulfilled by them!'

Anna's advice for life is typically sage: 'Just take life as it is. Italian cooking leads to a comfortable life, and a bonus: longevity! Eat well, play well, and laugh a lot. Conviviality is the heart of life!'

Chicken Thighs Braised in Cider w/ Sweet Potatoes
By Neven Maguire

'This recipe has to be one of my all-time favourites, one that I find myself returning to again and again. It has tons of flavour but takes very little time to get in the oven compared to traditional casseroles. Ask any good butcher to prepare the chicken thighs for you, I think they are so much more succulent than chicken breasts' — *Neven*

This recipe has been kindly donated by Neven Maguire, leading chef and owner of The MacNean Restaurant.

Ingredients

12 rindless streaky bacon rashers
12 boneless, skinless chicken thighs
3 tablespoons Donegal rapeseed oil
2 onions, cut into wedges
2 sweet potatoes, peeled and cut into cubes
2 garlic cloves, crushed

275g (10oz) flat mushrooms, sliced
2 tablespoons redcurrant jelly
Finely grated rind of 1 orange
1 bay leaf
450ml (¾ pint) chicken stock
120ml (4fl oz) dry cider
2 teaspoons fresh thyme leaves

1 tablespoon chopped fresh flat-leaf parsley
1 tablespoon toasted flaked almonds
Sea salt and freshly ground black pepper
Creamy mashed potatoes, to serve

Method

1. Preheat the oven to 200C/400F/Gas mark 6.

2. Stretch each rasher with the back of a table knife, then wrap each one around a chicken thigh.

3. Heat the oil in a large casserole dish with a lid and cook the wrapped chicken thighs in batches until lightly browned all over. Arrange on a plate and set aside.

4. Reduce the heat, then add the onions and sweet potatoes and sauté for 5 minutes, until golden.

5. Add the garlic and cook for 1 minute, stirring to prevent the mixture from sticking.

6. Add the mushrooms, redcurrant jelly, orange rind and bay leaf, then pour in the stock and cider.

7. Bring to the boil, then reduce the heat and return the chicken to the casserole and stir in the thyme.

8. Cover and cook in the oven for 1 hour, until the chicken is completely tender and the sauce has thickened slightly. Season to taste and stir in the parsley.

9. To serve, sprinkle the casserole with the flaked almonds, then place directly on the table with a large bowl of creamy mashed potatoes to mop up all those delicious juices.

Frank's American Green Bean Casserole
By May Casey

May's son, Frank, couldn't cook until he went to America, where he worked in several restaurants as a student. Later he became the main chef for his young family and this recipe is the result of many experiments with them.

Preparation time 15 minutes *Cooking time* 40 minutes
Equipment 25cm/10 inch ovenproof dish *Serves* 4-6

Ingredients

60g/2oz butter
1 large onion
110g/4oz Portobello mushrooms
250g/8oz sliced green beans

150ml/¼ pint chicken stock
1 can condensed mushroom soup
100g/3oz Parmesan cheese, grated

Salt and pepper to taste
French-fried onion strings for topping*

Method

1. Preheat the oven to 180C/350F/Gas mark 4.

2. Melt the butter in a large pan, and sauté the onions and mushrooms until soft.

3. Boil the green beans in the chicken stock for 2 minutes and drain.

4. Combine the green beans, mushroom soup, onions, and mushrooms and season to taste. Stir well.

5. Pour into the greased baking dish.

6. Top the casserole with the Parmesan and onion strings and bake for 15-20 minutes, or until the casserole is hot and the cheese is melted.

*French-fried onion strings can be bought canned in America but they can be easily made by dipping thinly-sliced onion rings in batter and deep-frying for about 3 minutes until golden.

Beef Casserole
By Sarah Doherty

This casserole can be made ahead of time and reheated. The long, slow cooking delivers incredibly tender meat.

Preparation time 20 minutes *Cooking time* 3-3½ hours
Equipment Large casserole dish with lid *Serves* 4-6

Ingredients

1 tablespoon vegetable oil
1 tablespoon butter
2 celery stalks, thickly sliced
1 onion, chopped
2 large carrots halved lengthways, then cut into thick slices
1 bay leaf
3 sprigs thyme
2 tablespoons plain flour

2 tablespoons tomato purée
2 tablespoons Worcestershire sauce
2 beef stock cubes, crumbled
600ml hot water
850g stewing beef (featherblade or brisket works nicely), cut into nice large chunks

Method

1. Preheat the oven to 160C/325F/Gas mark 3.

2. Heat the oil and butter in the casserole dish.

3. Put the celery, onion, carrots, bay leaf and a sprig thyme into a pan on a medium heat and stir.

4. Soften for 10 minutes then stir in the flour for 1 minute

5. Add the tomato purée, Worcestershire sauce and beef stock cubes.

6. Gradually stir in 600ml hot water, then tip in the beef and bring to a gentle simmer.

7. Cover and put in the oven for 2½ hours.

8. Uncover and cook for 30-60 minutes or longer, until the meat is really tender and the sauce is thickened.

Sarah, or 'Ally' as she is known, from her childhood name Ally Kershaw, was born on Christmas Eve and her brother, Noel, a year later on New Year's Eve. Their close ages meant they were destined to be pals. As children they often spent summer holidays together in their Granny's in Offaly. Later, as a young adult, Sarah was often to be found working on Noel's allotment and cultivating vegetables for her family, a place that fostered her love of good food.

Following her second job in Twilford's Tailoring, where she was a presser, Sarah met and married the love of her life, 'the jolly, smiling and already a cook' Paddy Doherty. Paddy had never been far from Sarah, growing up around the corner and being a firm fixture in the local 'cowboy' band as a singer. In fact it might have been Paddy's cowboy hat she fell in love with first!

They went on to have two children; David, their first born, and Suzanne, who they adopted from a nearby convent. Sarah recalls that at the time they were lucky to be able to partition one of their rooms in two to meet the conditions of the adoption of their beloved daughter.

On a typical Saturday, whilst Paddy prepared the dinner, Sarah would go to her favourite place, Mount Argus church. When she returned, the family would have dinner together, happy in each other's company and so it has continued.

Rob's Rib-Eye Steak with Garlic Butter

By Robbie Phelan

A favourite romantic-evening meal for Robbie.

Preparation time 5 minutes *Cooking time* 45 minutes *Equipment* Baking tray *Serves* 2

Ingredients

2 rib-eye steaks,
about 2cm/1 inch thick
Salt and pepper to season
1 tablespoon oil

1 tablespoon butter
2 sprigs thyme
2 sprigs rosemary

2 cloves garlic, crushed
Baby potatoes and vegetables
of your choice for serving

Method

1. Preheat the oven to 120C/250F/Gas mark ½.

2. Season the steaks evenly on all sides with the salt and pepper.

3. Place the steaks on a wire rack on top of a baking sheet.

4. Bake for 35 minutes in the oven.

5. Heat the oil in a pan over a high heat until smoking.

6. Sear the steaks on each side for 30 seconds then remove from the pan.

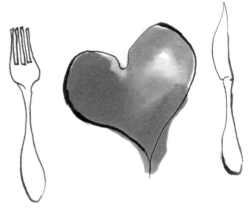

7. Immediately add the butter, thyme, rosemary, and garlic, and shake the pan to melt the butter quickly.

8. Place the butter and herbs on top of the steaks and move the steaks to the back of the pan.

9. Using a spoon, scoop the butter continuously over the steaks for about 30 seconds; this helps to cook the steak faster.

10. For a medium- or well-done steak, cook for a little longer.

11. Rest the steak on a cutting-board for 10 minutes, then slice and serve with baby potatoes and vegetables of your choice.

Dublin Coddle 1

By Christina Lyng

We have two 'Dublin Coddles' in this edition – try both and pick your own favourite.

Preparation time 20 minutes *Cooking time* 40 minutes
Equipment Large saucepan *Serves* 2

Ingredients

8-12 pork sausages
225g/½lb bacon pieces or approximately 8 rashers
6 medium-sized potatoes

2 medium onions
100g/4oz pearl barley
Pepper and salt to taste

Method

1. Wash, peel and chop the potatoes into 2cm/½ inch chunks.

2. Peel and chop the onions.

3. Place the sausages, bacon, potatoes, onions, and pearl barley into a large saucepan.

4. Season with salt and pepper.

5. Add enough cold water to just cover the ingredients.

6. Place on a high heat and bring to the boil.

7. Lower the heat and simmer for 30 minutes.

8. Ladle into soup bowls and add more seasoning if required.

9. Serve with crusty bread and plenty of butter.

Christina was the eldest of five sisters and one brother. Her father was the scholar of the family and taught her elocution. She recalls sitting in a small chair beside him for an hour every day until she learned to say 'pillow' and 'fellow' instead of 'pilla' and 'fella'. This gift enabled her to grow in confidence. Her mother was known as the 'Handywoman' of the family and was a hugely positive and formative influence on the family. She taught Christina not to be judgmental and to never hold a grudge. She instilled in her the lightness of spirit, buoyancy, and hopefulness that are traits she cherishes to this day.

These values helped her enormously when she settled in Birmingham in the 70s with her husband Bobby. After the bombings, they made an effort to keep talking, keep greeting people, and stay positive and open-minded. As a result of this attitude Christina says that they met the most wonderful people during that time.

Life wasn't always easy but Christina's faith has sustained her throughout hard times. When her baby son was born premature, her grandmother sent her a relic of Mother Mary Aikenhead. She taped it to his incubator to protect him and happily went on to have five more children.

Many years later, when Christina went to the hospice herself she was able to visit the Mother Mary Aikenhead memorial. There she thanked her for her precious son's life, and for the loving care all receive from the Hospice.

Dublin Coddle 2

By Christina O'Callaghan

There are hundreds of recipes for Dublin Coddle. This is the second one in this book but Christina believes hers is the original one!

Preparation time 10 minutes *Cooking time* 40 minutes
Equipment Medium-large saucepan *Serves* 4-6

Ingredients

350g/12oz waxy potatoes, peeled and cut into 2cm/¾ inch pieces

200g/7oz onion, chopped

225g/8oz sausages

600ml/1 pint chicken stock

Salt and pepper to taste

250g/9oz boiled bacon, cut into 2cm/½ inch pieces

1 tablespoon finely chopped fresh parsley

Method

1. Put the potatoes, onions, sausages, and stock into a saucepan.

2. Bring to the boil and simmer for about 30 minutes.

3. Add the bacon and cook for a further 10 minutes.

4. Place in serving bowls and sprinkle with the chopped parsley.

Given the recipe supplied, it's no surprise that Christina is a Dublin girl through and through. She was born on the South Circular Road, moved to Darley Street and then lived in Walkinstown.

When she grew up her first job was hard and badly paid, so she went to work for Jacobs. She wore gloves in the job interview to hide an injured hand from a childhood accident but on starting the job soon realised she was going to come up against difficulties. Her supervisor noticed her predicament and thankfully transferred Christina to the job of biscuit checker, where she worked happily for eight years, saving up as much as she could to buy a house.

When her mother became ill and she handed in her notice she was told she was foolish to forfeit her pension but her mother was always her first priority. Christina never married because she stayed at home looking after her mother and then her brother for over twenty-seven years. Despite this she didn't miss out on life. She and her brother had great times together; going to the Concert Hall or to the theatre, and always enjoyed a good meal out beforehand. People sometimes say 'you'll always find a friend in Dublin' and Christina is the exemplification of this. She is a cheerful, bright and friendly woman, ready for a chat and a laugh whenever possible.

Sausage-Meat Lasagne

By Gemma Rafter

Gemma professes not to cook, but this is her most-shared recipe and always goes down a treat. Try changing the cheese you use in the recipe each time for a different flavour.

Preparation time 25 minutes *Cooking time* 30 minutes
Equipment 25cm/10 inch square ovenproof dish, or similar *Serves* 4

Ingredients

250g/8oz sausage-meat
1 medium onion
1 clove garlic
1 pepper, sliced
250g/8oz mushrooms, sliced
1 small tin sweetcorn, drained

120g jar tomato pesto
400g tin chopped tomatoes
250g/8oz spinach leaves, chopped
250g/8oz crème fraiche
1 teaspoon brown sugar

12 sheets lasagne
100g/4oz cheese, grated (cheddar, gruyère, or any of your choice)

Method

1. Preheat the oven to 180C/350F/Gas mark 4.

2. Break up and fry the sausage-meat for 4-5 minutes.

3. Remove from the pan and set aside.

4. Fry the onion, garlic and pepper together in the same pan for 3-4 minutes.

5. Add the mushrooms and corn, and then stir in the pesto and tomatoes.

6. Mix well to combine all the ingredients.

7. Remove from the heat and stir in the sausage-meat, spinach leaves, crème fraiche, and sugar.

8. Spread one-third of the mixture over the base of the ovenproof dish.

9. Cover with lasagne sheets.

10. Repeat the layering, ending with sausage-meat mixture on top.

11. Bake in the oven for 30 minutes until the edges are beginning to bubble.

12. Sprinkle with the grated cheese and return to the oven for 10 minutes or until the cheese is golden and bubbling.

13. Serve with a salad of your choice and garlic bread.

Chicken and Bacon Casserole

By Paul Reid

This family casserole recipe was much loved by Paul's mother.

Preparation time 20 minutes *Cooking time* 90 minutes
Equipment Large casserole dish *Serves* 6-8

Ingredients

1 tablespoon cooking oil	chicken pieces (breast, leg, thigh)
2 large onions	150g/6oz plain flour
5 cloves garlic, crushed	2 chicken stock cubes
4 sprigs thyme or rosemary, finely chopped	6-8 carrots (500g approximately)
500g/1lb large chunks of smoked bacon	Salt and pepper to taste
1kg/2lbs large chunks of mixed	1 litre water

Method

1. Preheat the oven to 160C/325F/Gas mark 3.

2. Heat a large casserole dish on the hob.

3. Add the oil, onions, garlic and herbs, and cook on a medium heat until soft but not brown.

4. Add the smoked bacon and cook for 5 minutes

5. Add the chicken and cook for a further 5 minutes.

6. Add the flour and stock cubes to the casserole and mix to coat the meat.

7. Cook the flour in for 3-4 minutes, stirring all the time to prevent any sticking to the dish.

8. Slowly add 1 litre of water, mixing to avoid lumps.

9. Add the carrots, put the lid on the dish, and place in the preheated oven for 75 minutes.

10. Remove from the oven and serve with mashed potatoes and fresh greens.

As a boy, Paul lived in a Georgian redbrick house in Phibsboro. The kitchen - the centre of all activity - was painted vanilla white, with an old grey slab floor and red oil cloth on the table. It was also the room that housed his dog Patch, a Jack Russell with imploring brown eyes and floppy ears. Paul fondly remembers spending time here with his mother as a child. She would have lit the fire in the big range and she, Paul and Patch would listen together to BBC 4. She was very intelligent and thoughtful and, best of all, she adored Paul.

Paul was educated by the Christian Brothers, and revelled in Gaelic football, hurling, running, jumping hurdles and any and all forms of athletics. He was a popular boy and always involved in everything.

Paul's decision to move to the Hospice was a difficult one that took him 18 months to come to. However, since then he has found himself at ease. He has gone on to give lectures to medical students about his experience as someone in hospice care to assist their studies and it is clear that he is immensely popular still.

Crispy Mediterranean-style Chicken
By Lorna Rowe

This recipe was passed to Lorna from her Aunty Annie who loves Mediterranean food. It is a firm favourite because it is so tasty but very easy to make.

Preparation time **10 minutes** *Cooking time* **40 minutes** *Equipment* **Medium-sized casserole dish**
Serves **4**

Ingredients

150g/5oz sundried tomatoes	4 chicken fillets	25g/1oz parmesan cheese
150g/5oz roasted red peppers	50g/2oz breadcrumbs	Salt and pepper
2 cloves garlic, crushed	1 teaspoon butter	Oil for frying

Method

1. Preheat the oven to 180C/350F/Gas mark 4.
2. Lightly fry the chicken fillets for 5-6 minutes.
3. Blend the tomatoes, peppers and garlic in a food processor until combined.
4. Spread this sauce over the bottom of the casserole dish.
5. Place the chicken breasts on top and season with salt and pepper.
6. Sprinkle the breadcrumbs and parmesan cheese on top.
7. Dot the butter over the breadcrumbs
8. Bake in the preheated oven for 30 minutes.
9. Serve with rice, couscous, or quinoa.

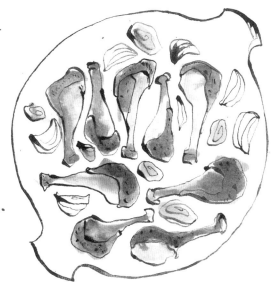

Lamb and Potato Casserole
By Sister Catherine

This hearty and wholesome casserole contains everything you need to provide a good balanced family dinner, all in one dish.

Preparation time 20 mins *Cooking time* 1 hour 40 minutes *Equipment* Large casserole dish *Serves* 4

Ingredients

4 leg of lamb steaks (750g/1½lbs) cut into bite-sized pieces

2 large onions, roughly chopped

2 celery sticks, roughly chopped

1 large carrot, peeled and roughly chopped

½ level tablespoon plain flour

½ tablespoon Worcestershire sauce

2 tablespoons tomato purée

225ml/8 fl oz good meat stock

1 bay leaf

500g/1lb potatoes, peeled and thinly sliced

A handful of parsley, finely chopped

Oil for frying

1 tablespoon butter

Method

1. Preheat the oven to 160C/225F/Gas mark 3.

2. In the casserole dish, fry the lamb in two batches for 3-4 minutes each, or until browned, then set aside.

3. Add the onions, celery and carrots to the pan and fry for 5 minutes.

4. Sprinkle over the flour and cook for a further 3 minutes.

5. Add the Worcestershire sauce, tomato purée and stock, bring to the boil.

6. Return the lamb to the dish and add the bay leaf.

7. Remove from the heat.

8. Arrange the sliced potatoes on top of the meat and vegetables.

9. Cover and cook in the preheated oven for 90 minutes, until the potatoes and lamb are tender.

10. Turn the temperature up to 200C/400F/Gas mark 6.

11. Dot the butter over the potato slices and cook for a further 10 minutes, uncovered, until the potatoes are golden.

12. Garnish with the parsley and serve.

13. For a lower-fat dish, the butter and oil can be substituted for low-calorie cooking spray

Chapter 4

Main Meals
Vegetarian & Fish

Mac and Cheese

By Rhoda Nolan

This recipe takes a simple American staple and elevates it to new heights.

Preparation time 20 minutes *Cooking time* 15 minutes
Equipment 25cm/10 inch casserole dish *Serves* 4

Ingredients

200g/8oz macaroni	¼ teaspoon dry mustard
4 tablespoons butter	100g/4oz cheddar cheese, grated
3 tablespoons plain flour	
1 small onion, finely chopped	50g/2oz Swiss cheese, grated
300ml/½ pint milk	6 tablespoons breadcrumbs
Salt and pepper	1 tablespoon parmesan

Method

1. Preheat the oven to 190C/375F/Gas mark 5.

2. Cook the macaroni according to the manufacturer's instructions.

3. Meanwhile, melt the butter, stir in the onions and cook for 3 minutes.

4. Add the flour and mix well.

5. Slowly add the milk, stirring with each addition to avoid lumps.

6. Season with salt, pepper and mustard.

7. Bring to the boil and stir until the sauce thickens.

8. Add the cheddar, Swiss cheese and cooked macaroni to the sauce, and mix thoroughly.

9. Pour into the casserole dish and sprinkle the breadcrumbs and parmesan cheese on top.

10. Bake in the preheated oven for 15 minutes until golden on top.

Rhoda was brought up in England and had the good fortune - she says so herself - to meet and marry an Irishman, Philip. Together they emigrated to New York City where she worked as a Cordon Bleu chef for eighteen years. Their children were born in the States and though they still live there, Rhoda and Philip returned to Kilkenny, Ireland where they launched the Fine Food Festival ten years ago. A lifetime of cooking, both for family and as a career, means Rhoda has collected many recipes on her journey and she is delighted to pass on a few of her favourites.

Every child in America knows Mac and Cheese. It comes in a packet, to which you just add milk to the powder to make the sauce and then stir in the cooked macaroni. Rhoda laughs at how it is the most amazing orange colour you have ever seen. This version she reassures us, however, is a much tastier one and certainly a more natural-looking colour!

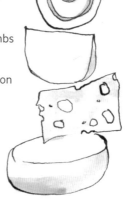

Smoked Salmon Bake

By Sylvia Doyle

This recipe has always been a success for Sylvia. She has been making it for years and it never fails to please.

Preparation time 30 minutes *Cooking time* 35 minutes
Equipment 25cm/10 inch square baking dish *Serves* 4-6

Ingredients

Oil for frying	500g/1lb smoked salmon
1 large onion, chopped	200g/7oz smoked rashers, lightly cooked
2 cloves garlic, crushed	
150g/6oz button mushrooms, sliced	500ml/1 pint cream
8 large potatoes	150g/6oz cheddar cheese, grated

Method

1. Preheat the oven to 180C/350F/Gas mark 4.

2. Put the oil in a pan and lightly fry the onions, garlic, and mushrooms for 3-4 minutes.

3. Peel and parboil the potatoes until slightly soft. Allow to cool.

4. Slice the potatoes thinly and layer on the bottom of the dish.

5. Next, place a layer of smoked salmon, bacon, onions, garlic and mushrooms on top.

6. Pour half the cream over and repeat the layers once more.

7. Finish with a layer of potatoes topped with the grated cheese.

8. Bake in the oven for 25 minutes until the potatoes are cooked and the cheese is browning and bubbling.

Sylvia has been in the Community Reablement Unit eight times, it helps her maintain her independence.

Sylvia is a small person and her mother used to say to her: 'There is nothing you can't do Sylvia. You are just small – otherwise you are just the same as the rest of us.' Sylvia points out all the adjustments the team in the CRU have made to her room and smiles, 'I am happy here.'

Sylvia has had four knee replacements. Before the last one she endured years of increasing disability and pain. Her surgeon discovered that her previous replacement had come loose and the metal was gouging into the bone. Lately, when she ruptured her knee, he installed a rotation hinge. 'Thank God you only have two knees!' he told her. She says that the combination of his dedication, compassion and her own good humour has saved her. Her motto for dealing with her treatment quickly became: 'you have the skill, I have the faith.'

Lately, Sylvia has had to draw a line under driving, it has become too difficult and so she has decided to sell her car, and put the money into taxis. Now, she says ruefully, 'I have to do this for Sylvia.' Sylvia doesn't do negative. 'I have to get my head around things,' she says, which is her code for dealing with things, thinking them through and coming to acceptance. Her nickname is 'Hawk-Eye'. She sees people's troubles and they open up to her or, as she good-naturedly explains it, 'I pat them down, then I puff them up!'

Chilli and Garlic Mussels with Pasta

By Deirdre Ryan

This is so tasty and very easy to prepare. The fresher the mussels the tastier the dish. Enjoy this as a perfect late supper served with a fresh green salad.

Preparation time 10 minutes *Cooking time* 20 minutes *Equipment* A large saucepan *Serves* 2

Ingredients

1kg mussels
1 tablespoon olive oil
5 shallots, peeled and finely chopped

1 garlic clove, peeled and crushed
Pinch of chilli flakes
400g tin chopped tomatoes
Salt and pepper to taste

300g/11oz linguine, or pasta of your choice
2 tablespoons flat-leafed parsley, chopped

Method

1. Place the mussels in a large bowl of cold water.

2. Scrub well to remove barnacles and pull away any beard.

3. Discard any mussels that are damaged or are open and won't close when tapped.

4. Heat the oil in a large saucepan over a medium heat.

5. Add the shallots, garlic, and chilli flakes, and cook for 2-3 minutes.

6. Add the tomatoes, then bring to the boil and simmer for 10 minutes.

7. Taste and then season with salt and pepper.

8. Cook the pasta according to the manufacturer's instructions.

9. Meanwhile, add the prepared mussels to the sauce and cook for 3-4 minutes.

10. Drain the pasta, reserving 2-3 tablespoons of the cooking liquid.

11. Return the pasta to the saucepan together with the reserved cooking liquid.

12. Pour the mussel mixture over the pasta and stir gently to combine all ingredients.

13. Place on a low heat and heat through.

14. Drizzle over a little olive oil and sprinkle with the chopped parsley.

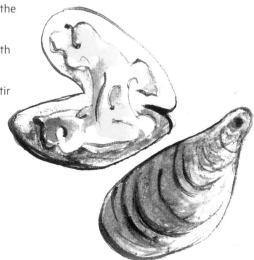

Homity Pie

By Trish Farrelly

Homity Pie is an open-topped pie said to have first been made by the Land-Girls during WW2.

Preparation time 15 minutes *Cooking time* 20-25 minutes
Equipment 25cm/10 inch pie dish *Serves* 4

Ingredients

Low calorie cooking spray
340g/12oz potatoes, peeled and cubed
225g/8oz onions, chopped
225g/8oz leeks, thinly sliced
198g/7oz frozen peas
2 garlic cloves, finely chopped

Handful fresh parsley, chopped
Handful fresh thyme, chopped
2 eggs, lightly beaten
85ml/2½fl oz vegetable stock
160g/6oz low-fat Cheddar cheese, grated
Salt and pepper to taste

Method

1. Preheat the oven to 220C/425F/Gas mark 7.

2. Spray the pie dish with low calorie cooking spray.

3. Boil the potatoes for 15-20 minutes until tender.

4. Drain the water off and return to the pan and mash them. Set aside until needed.

5. Spray a large, non-stick frying pan with the cooking spray and stir-fry the onions, leeks and peas over a medium heat for 6-8 minutes, or until the vegetables have softened.

6. Add the mashed potatoes, garlic, parsley, thyme, eggs, stock and half the cheese, season and stir to combine.

7. Spoon the mixture into the prepared ovenproof dish and scatter over the remaining cheese.

8. Bake in the preheated oven for 20 minutes or until golden brown and bubbling.

9. This tastes great served with a green salad.

Patricia worked at further education and training centre FÁS for many years. She was dedicated to her career but primarily it meant that she could earn money to take her family on excursions and trips abroad. She revelled in dozens of holidays in her favourite destination, Lanzarote.

A big draw for her on holidays was always having the time to read. An avid reader, Patricia has been a member of her local Book Club for twenty years. She is a confirmed book addict, and feels a profound pleasure in reading. She always has a book on the go and many more on her desk in her TBR (to-be-read) pile!

Drawing is also a big pleasure of hers. She enjoys painting pictures of cartoon characters. Her favourite is a smiling mouse with his travel bag slung over his shoulder on a stick, climbing over a cat who is blocking his pathway. The cat is stretched out, conveniently asleep in the sunshine!

Life's simple pleasures are many for Patricia. She looks forward to a cup of tea, talking to her neighbours, listening to music, being with her beautiful daughters and having a laugh with her brother, who makes her favourite soup every week and brings it for lunch. It's delicious but still not a patch on her famous Homity pie!

Smoked Salmon Pasta

By Pauline Foy

This recipe was discovered by Pauline many years ago in her local butcher's shop.

Preparation time 10 minutes *Cooking time* 20 minutes
Equipment Non-stick saucepan
Serves 2 as main course or 4 as starter

Ingredients

1 small onion
250g/8oz button mushrooms, halved
170ml/¼ pint fresh cream
1 tablespoon white wine

200g/7oz smoked salmon
Handful fresh basil
Salt and pepper
200g/7oz dried pasta of your choice

Method

1. Heat the oil in a non-stick saucepan and lightly fry the onion until transparent.

2. Add the mushrooms and cook for 3 minutes.

3. Add the cream, then rinse the cream carton or container with the white wine before adding it to the pan.

4. Simmer gently for 2-3 minutes to reduce and season to taste.

5. Cook the pasta according to the manufacturer's instructions and drain.

6. Add the smoked salmon and basil to the sauce and stir in.

7. Combine the sauce and pasta and serve immediately on warm plates.

Pauline loves a chat. 'I can talk for Ireland!' she happily explains. She tells how she recently broke her hip and spent time in the Community Reablement Unit of the Hospice. 'I love the nurses; they are so caring,' she smiles. She has a great sense of humour and her advice for anyone who is older is short, sweet and typically amusing: 'don't turn around too fast!'

She has her sadness too however. She lost her husband Bob unexpectedly and grieved for years. She says that the happiest memory of her life was her wedding day in July. Everyone was on their bikes, waving to her, as they followed the happy couple in the taxi. She wore a shining brocade wedding dress and short veil decorated with rose leaves.

Despite her loss, Pauline says she feels lucky. She is delighted that her son Robert lives with her. Every night they have dinner on folding tables in the living room, chat about the day and watch the news. It is the simple pleasures they enjoy together that sustain her.

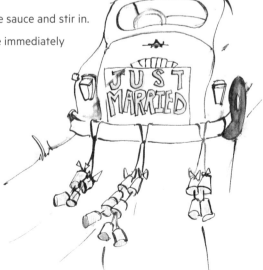

Shepherdless Pie
By Eilish Byrne

A great name for a delicious meat-free Shepherd's Pie!

Preparation time 30 minutes *Cooking time* 90- 95 mins (using raw split peas) *Equipment* Medium casserole dish *Serves* 6-8

Ingredients

450g/16oz split peas (or 2 tins ready-cooked split peas)

Oil for frying

2 onions, diced

4 cloves garlic, crushed

2 carrots

2 sticks celery

1 parsnip

8 medium-sized mushrooms

1 vegetable stock pot

1 litre/2 pints water

2 tablespoons fresh mixed herbs (parsley, sage, rosemary, thyme)

Salt and pepper to taste

1kg/2lbs potatoes

100g butter

50ml milk

2 tablespoons fresh chives

100g/4oz grated cheddar cheese

Method

1. Rinse the split peas under running water.
2. Heat 2 tablespoons of oil in a large saucepan. Add the onions and garlic and gently fry until soft and translucent.
3. Add the split peas. Pour in the water, bring to the boil and skim off any white scum that appears on the surface.
4. Turn the heat down and simmer gently with a lid on the pan for 45–60 minutes.
5. Meanwhile, peel and chop all the vegetables.
6. Put a tablespoon of oil into another saucepan and fry the vegetables, stirring all the time.
7. Add the mixed herbs and salt and pepper and stir well.
8. Add the stock pot and a small amount of water and cook on a low heat until the vegetables are tender, about 30 minutes.
9. Preheat the oven to 180C/350F/Gas mark 4.
10. Boil and mash the potatoes with the milk and butter. Add the chives.
11. Put the split peas and vegetables into the casserole dish. Place the mashed potatoes on top.
12. Sprinkle the grated cheese over the potato and cook in the oven for 30-40 minutes until the potato and cheese are bubbling and golden.

A serious car accident in 1972 changed everything for Eilish. While recovering in hospital she had what she describes as 'a classic out-of-body experience.' 'I was up high, looking down at myself... the experience was ethereal, airy, but most of all very peaceful. Now I have no fear of death.'

Dealing with her injuries taught her valuable lessons. She learned that anything creative takes you away from your brooding. She discovered the benefits of meditation for alleviating depression and learned to 'mind her mind.' When asked how she deals with her injuries Eilish is mindful in her response: 'You need honesty, compassion, love, kindness and tolerance. You need to decide to keep the constant thought of others as a normal state of mind. Then, you will be surprised to discover that you feel happy!'

Her motto is 'this too will pass' and she reminds herself of it when she feels overwhelming sadness. For her there is nowhere else in Ireland like the Hospice.

Chapter 5

Desserts

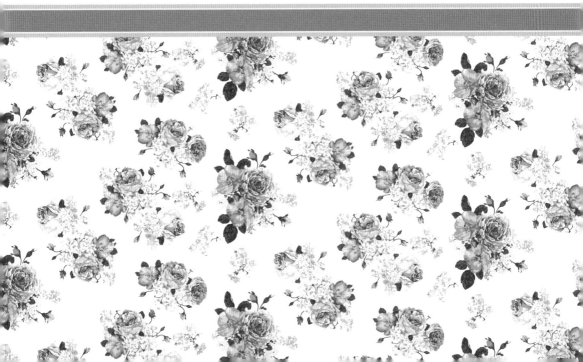

Classic Tiramisu

By Mary Mansfield

This classic Italian dessert can be made with or without the addition of a drop of whiskey or brandy.

Preparation time 20 minutes *Chilling time* 3-5 hours or overnight
Equipment 25cm/10 inch oblong sandwich plate *Serves* 6-8

Ingredients

2 teaspoons instant coffee granules
125ml/¼ pint hot water
20-30 boudoir/sponge fingers
2 large eggs, separated
50g/2oz caster sugar
500g/18oz cream cheese (mascarpone is delicious)
250ml/½ pint double cream
3 teaspoons cocoa powder
Grated chocolate to decorate

Method

1. Mix together the coffee and hot water.

2. Arrange the sponge fingers side-by-side along the length of the sandwich or serving plate.

3. Sprinkle half of the coffee mixture over the sponge fingers.

4. Whisk the egg yolks, cream cheese, sugar and double cream together until smooth.

5. Whisk the egg whites separately until stiff.

6. Then, gently fold the egg whites into the cream cheese mixture.

7. Cover the sponge fingers with this cream cheese mixture and then place another layer of sponge fingers on top. Drizzle the rest of the coffee mixture over the top.

8. Refrigerate for 3-5 hours or overnight.

9. Just before serving, dust the dessert with the cocoa powder and decorate with grated chocolate.

10. For an adult version of this dessert replace the hot water with whiskey or brandy for a special treat.

Mary celebrated 58 years of marriage this year but sadly a few months later she lost her precious husband. They were very happy together and never spent a day apart. They were inseparable, when you saw one, you saw the other. It was a heart-breaking loss for Mary.

Her grief affects her deeply and she finds comfort and strength in prayer. Mary knows how to look on the brighter side of life thankfully. She has always been a happy person, always the kind of person who kept busy, was never idle. She values immensely the love and comfort she receives from her children and her neighbours. They look after her and make her happy. Despite the pain and challenges she has ensured she is always on the go and will always find something to do to keep her busy. Even now she says: 'Gardening was my hobby, and I can still go out and pull a few weeds, can't I? Sure, what more could I want?'

Mary has huge praise for the care she has received from the staff in the Hospice's Community Reablement Unit. She was delighted to provide this recipe and hopes you enjoy her Tiramisu as much as she does.

Speedy Banoffee

By Alice Victory

This is the fastest ever Banoffee in the West!

Preparation time 70 minutes *Chilling time:* 30 minutes
Equipment 23cm/9 inch loose-bottomed pie dish *Serves* 6-8

Ingredients

250g/8oz digestive biscuits	4 small bananas
100g/4oz butter, melted	250ml/½ pint fresh cream
390g/14oz can caramel	Grated chocolate for decoration

Method

1. Line the tin with parchment paper to prevent the cold biscuit mixture from sticking.

2. Place the biscuits in a strong plastic bag and crush with a rolling pin.

3. Combine the biscuits with the melted butter until the mixture is moist.

4. Press the biscuit mixture into the base of the tin and chill for 30 minutes until firm and set.

5. Spread the caramel over the base with a spoon or spatula.

6. Slice the bananas and arrange on top of the caramel.

7. Whip the fresh cream and spread over the caramel and bananas.

8. Decorate with grated chocolate.

9. Leave in the fridge until required. This dessert will keep well for up to two days.

Alice wasn't always a great baker. She remembers, ruefully, her first time making Banoffee pie using a can of condensed milk, before cans of caramel were available to buy. She accidentally left it on the stove for far too long and it exploded everywhere – even making a hole in the kitchen ceiling! Ever the optimist, she simply got new cupboards, new curtains, a new floor ... and tried again.

Referring to such domestic and other tragedies, she says: 'Nothing would best me.' When she made her first cherry cake, the cherries dropped straight through to the bottom. So, it became a new kind of dessert, one she named 'Upside Down Cherry Delight.' However, despite the somewhat steep culinary learning curve, her cakes have always sold out in the school bake sales!

Bakewell Tart

By Elaine Payne

The delicious combination of almonds and jam make this recipe a firm family favourite for decades.

Preparation time 30 minutes *Cooking time* 35-40 minutes
Equipment 30 x 20cm/12 x 8 inch Swiss roll tin, greased and lined, baking beads *Serves* 8-10

Ingredients

Pastry
300g/10½oz plain flour, plus extra for dusting
125g/4oz cold unsalted butter, cut into cubes
30g/1oz sugar
2 large free-range eggs
2 tablespoons milk

Filling
225g/8oz unsalted butter, softened
225g/8oz caster sugar
225g/8oz ground almonds
3 free-range eggs
1 lemon, finely grated zest only
50g/2oz plain flour
350g raspberry jam
Flaked almonds, for sprinkling

Method

1. Rub the butter into the flour and sugar until the mixture resembles breadcrumbs. Add one egg and mix to form a rough dough.

2. Roll out the pastry and line the tin with it, chill in the fridge for 30 minutes.

3. Preheat the oven to 200C/400F/Gas mark 6.

4. Line the chilled tart case with greaseproof paper and fill with baking beans. Bake for 15-20 minutes until lightly golden-brown.

5. Remove the paper and beans and brush with the remaining beaten egg. Return to the oven for a further 5 minutes, until golden-brown.

6. Turn the oven down to 180C/350F/Gas mark 4.

7. Beat the butter and sugar together until pale and fluffy. Mix in the ground almonds, then crack in the three eggs, one at a time, beating well. Fold in the lemon zest and the flour.

8. Spread the raspberry jam across the base of the cooled pastry, leaving a small gap around the edge. Spread the filling mixture over the jam and sprinkle over the flaked almonds.

9. Bake for 20 minutes until the filling is set and golden-brown.

Elaine grew up on a busy but happy farm and recalls her mother having 'a Dr. Dolittle approach' to the farm animals; all the pigs were known by name and as a child Elaine would hitch a lift on the back of the free-range pigs until gently bumped off.

It was during this idyllic childhood that she began to realize that enjoying the beautiful sights of nature might become more than just a pastime. Looking at fields of sunflowers, rows of daffodils, or rosy piglets with their mothers became a visual treasure and she began to try to capture the sights in her knitting and stitching.

Elaine iterates just how important the Hospice has been for her. She is certain she would not be so well, so advanced in her recovery, without the support and encouragement of the staff, in particular the Occupational Therapy nurses.

Elaine feels it's so important to her to give heart and cheer to others. If she can make a small difference to anyone's day she feels lucky. Her energy and drive come from her spirituality and she passes on blessings in her wool, her work, and her words: 'When love is in you, you give it out.'

21st Century Bread and Butter Pudding
By Amy Collins

This is a beautifully light and tasty alternative to the traditional version of this dessert. Replacing the bread with hot cross buns, panettone, or brioche gives a very European flavour. This recipe complements our Easy Pavlova recipe, as it uses the egg yolks left over from making the meringue.

Preparation time 10 minutes, plus 1 hour resting *Cooking time* 45-60 minutes
Equipment 25cm/10 inch ovenproof dish *Serves* 6-8

Ingredients

5 or 6 hot cross buns, or 10 slices panettone or brioche
100g/4oz butter, softened

3 large egg yolks, beaten
250ml/½ pint double cream
50ml/2fl oz of milk

50g/2oz sultanas
To serve:
Cream, ice cream, or both!

Method

1. Preheat the oven to 180C/350°F/Gas mark 4.

2. Cut the hot cross buns, panettone or brioche into thin slices.

3. Spread the slices with butter then arrange them to cover the base of the ovenproof dish.

4. Sprinkle the sultanas over the top.

5. In a bowl, beat the egg yolks, cream, and milk together, and pour this mixture over the slices of bread.

6. Let the mixture rest for around 30-60 minutes.

7. Bake in the oven for about 45-60 minutes until the custard has set.

8. Marmalade can be added to the bread or 2 tablespoons of brandy or whiskey to the cream for an extra kick.

German Apple Pie

By Mary Williams

This pie is delicious served hot with custard for dessert or cold with a cup of coffee.

Preparation time 15 minutes *Cooking time* 45-50 minutes
Equipment 18cm/7 inch round pie dish or tin, greased *Serves* 6-8

Ingredients

150g/5oz butter	2 eggs, beaten
225g/8oz plain flour	600g/1lb 5oz cooking apples,
Pinch of salt	peeled and sliced
175g/6oz caster sugar	75g/2oz brown sugar

Method

1. Preheat the oven to 220C/425F/Gas mark 7.

2. Melt the butter in a large saucepan then remove from the heat.

3. Add the flour, salt, sugar and beaten eggs to the melted butter.

4. Mix to a firm dough, then roll out into two pieces, large enough to fit the pie tin.

5. Place half of the rolled dough in the tin and layer the apples evenly on top.

6. Sprinkle the brown sugar over the top of the pie.

7. Place the remaining rolled sheet of dough over the apples and pinch the edges to the base to seal the pie shut.

8. Bake in the preheated oven for 10 minutes.

9. Reduce the temperature to 180C/350F/Gas mark 4 and bake for a further 35-40 minutes.

10. Remove from the oven and serve either hot or cold with cream or custard.

During Lent each Spring, mass would be said in a local house, which was a great honour for the selected family. On one occasion Mary's home was chosen as this privileged location. In preparation the house had to be spruced up, cleaned and painted. There was a great deal of anticipation and planning for the event and the family were joined by neighbours and friends so a festive atmosphere would prevail.

The altar was set up in the sitting room, with all the trimmings of a church altar. Family and friends gathered in the kitchen-dining room, a large homely room framed by a picture window. The window looked out on the two-mile long sandy beach outside, surrounded by a fringe of navy purple and blue Kerry Mountains rolling across the bay.

A cooked breakfast was first served to the priest, then lunch, and once the formalities were over 30-40 family and friends continued the party. Patch, the family's Lakeland terrier, was always to be found at any event as food was plentiful. He would eagerly place his little paw on her knee, showing his love and perhaps even inviting her to share her slice of pie with him. This delicious German Apple Pie was a real treat and was always served on the best Wedgewood plates, and eaten almost as quickly as it could be dished out.

Peach Cobbler

By Rhoda Nolan

This homely, juicy sweet dessert is the ultimate flavour of summer.

Preparation time 10 minutes *Cooking time* 60 minutes
Equipment A large pie dish *Serves* 4-6

Ingredients

450g/1lb ripe peaches, peeled and sliced
450g/1lb soft brown sugar
100g/4oz butter
150g/6oz plain flour

1 teaspoon baking powder
Pinch of salt
235ml/9fl oz milk
Ice cream or fresh cream to serve

Method

1. Preheat the oven to 180C/350F/Gas mark 4.

2. Mix the peaches with half the sugar and set aside.

3. Melt the butter in the pie dish.

4. Beat the rest of the sugar, the flour, baking powder, salt and milk into a batter in a mixing bowl.

5. Pour this mixture over the melted butter in the pie dish.

6. Place the sugared peaches on top of the batter. Do NOT stir.

7. Bake in the preheated oven for 60 minutes.

8. The batter will rise to the top and will be brown and crisp when the cobbler is done.

9. Serve warm with whipped cream or ice cream

ever trust a clean cookbook.
Rhoda's cooking bible is The *Joy of Cooking* written by Irma Rombauer and printed in 1931. Irma's daughter, Marion wrote about Irma in this way: 'How grateful I am for her buoyant example, for the strong feeling of roots she gave me, for her conviction that, well grounded, you can make the most of life, no matter what it brings.'

This philosophy is one that Rhoda understands applies to the art of cooking. Be firm about knowing your ingredients, understand how to handle them and study how to enjoy preparing good, wholesome and delightful food. Be meticulous about the foods we eat, the foods we heat, the foods we keep.

For three years Rhoda and her family lived in Atlanta, Georgia. Atlanta is a place wonderfully steeped in history, and with charming people. This recipe is the South's version of Peach Cobbler. It is nothing like the recipe used in Ireland as this version has a scone-based top and is so simple. 'Oh,' and 'by the way,' Rhoda adds... 'My *Joy of Cooking* book is frayed, dog-eared and the pages are covered in stains and drips.'

Dad's Apple Dumplings

By Mary Kirwan

When Mary's Dad was growing up with his seven siblings in Wexford in the 50's, goods may have been scarce but there were always apples aplenty from the garden. His mother used every last one for stewed apples, baked apples, apple tart, or his favourite of all, apple dumplings.

Preparation time 30 minutes *Cooking time* 50-60 minutes
Equipment A large oven-proof baking dish *Serves* 6

Ingredients

Pastry:
225g/8oz plain flour
125g/4oz butter
1 tablespoon sugar

1 large egg, beaten
1 tablespoon cold water
Filling:
6 apples, peeled and cored

1 tablespoon brown sugar per apple
1 pinch of cinnamon per apple
1 pinch nutmeg per apple
1 teaspoon butter per apple

Method

1. Place the butter in the freezer for about 15 minutes to harden.

2. Sieve the flour into a bowl.

3. Grate the butter into the flour, you may need a little flour on your fingers for this.

4. Using the tips of your fingers, rub the grated butter into the flour.

5. Add the sugar and mix well.

6. Add sufficient beaten egg to the mixture to make a soft dough.

7. Turn the pastry onto a floured board and roll it out into a large rectangle.

8. Cut the rectangle into 6 squares and roll each square out until it is large enough to cover one whole apple.

9. Place one apple on each pastry square with the cored opening facing upwards.

10. Place the butter and half the sugar in the opening, then sprinkle the cinnamon and nutmeg on top. Place the rest of the sugar around the apple.

11. Bring the opposite corners of the pastry square together and pinch gently to seal using wet fingertips, repeat with the remaining corners.

12. Ensure all the sides of the dough are pinched together to completely seal in the apple.

13. Repeat with the other apples.

14. Place the six apples in the prepared baking dish and bake in the preheated oven for 50-60 minutes.

15. To serve, place each apple dumpling in a dessert bowl and spoon some ice cream over the top.

Apple Slab Cake
By Patricia O'Donovan

This recipe was passed down to Patricia from her mother, Ellie Barry.

Preparation time 15 minutes *Cooking time* 20 minutes
Equipment 20cm/8 inch pie dish, greased *Serves* 4-6

Ingredients

280g/10oz butter
454g/1lb self-raising flour
2 tbsp sugar
1 level tsp salt
2 medium eggs, beaten

680g/1½lb apples, stewed with 75g/3oz sugar
Custard, fresh cream, or ice cream to serve

Method

1. Preheat the oven to 190C/375F/Gas mark 5.

2. Rub the butter into the flour until it resembles fine breadcrumbs.

3. Mix in the sugar and salt.

4. Combine this mixture with the egg to make a stiff dough, reserve a little of the egg for glazing.

5. Add a little water if necessary to draw the dough together.

6. Roll out the dough and line the pie dish with half of it.

7. Spread a thick layer of the stewed apple over the dough.

8. Roll the remainder of the dough out on a floured surface and place over the stewed apple.

9. Brush the top of the dough with the beaten egg to glaze.

10. Bake in the oven for 20 minutes, until light golden brown on top.

Patricia's mother, Ellie Barry, ran a pub in Cork. As a child Patricia spent the summers in Glengariff, in the family home of their barmaid, Margaret Dorney, on their large and happy farm.

Life there was idyllic; exploring all the outhouses, visiting the pigs, horses and hens every morning, rearing and growing food. The fields all had names: 'Nano's Parkeen', 'Tay Daly's Field', 'The Inch', and 'The Bog' and through them Patricia's adventure and imagination ran wild.

This kind of idyllic youth couldn't last forever and at age 19 Patricia went to Paris to work as an au pair. Arriving home, polished and with good French, she proceeded to get a job in Douglas Loane's jewellery shop in Cobh. She joined an acting group, and remembers her first role in 'The Stranger.' For this role, she was dressed fabulously and richly, decorated with real jewellery loaned to her from the shop. It was happily through her involvement in theatre that she met her husband Jim and then family became her new happy place.

An illness suffered in 1985 marked a defining change in her life. She became ill after attending a dinner in Glyndebourne and was eventually diagnosed with Lysteria. It took her two years to recover and taught her a lot about living in the moment. She recalls Jim's devotion in caring for her throughout it, even taking her in a wheelchair to the Canaries for a holiday.

Patricia feels that older people have a responsibility to 'Give something back'. Her advice is: 'Look outside yourself, form relationships with anyone and everyone, no matter who, when or where. Stay in the moment and savour life right now.'

Rapid Raspberry Trifle

By Angela Curran

There's something so nostalgic about trifle, everyone loves this childhood dessert. The raspberries make this a real summertime dessert but you can easily substitute them for other berries or fruits that are in season.

Preparation time 10 minutes *Cooking time* 5 minutes
Equipment Round glass trifle bowl *Serves* 4-6

Ingredients

50g/2oz almonds
1 Madeira cake,
20cm/8 inch square
225g/8oz frozen raspberries
75g/3oz sugar to sweeten
raspberries

100ml/6 tablespoons sweet sherry
250ml/½ pint fresh cream
50g/2oz glacé cherries, halved

Method

1. Place the almonds on a baking sheet and toast under the grill until light brown.

2. Slice the cake into 2cm/½ inch pieces and place at the bottom of the trifle bowl.

3. Sprinkle the sweet sherry over the cake.

4. Place the raspberries in a saucepan with the sugar and simmer for 5 minutes.

5. When cool, pour the raspberry mixture over the cake.

6. Cover with the whipped cream and sprinkle the toasted almonds on top.

7. Decorate with the glacé cherries.

Angela was born in Ilford, Essex during WW2. She remembers the whine of bombs and hiding fearfully in her local air raid shelter. She remembers scarlet fever being just as bad.

She lived in Edinburgh for the next fifteen years and met her husband there. After marriage she moved to Cork, where she went on to have five precious children. Nothing, not even a war, could have prepared Angela for what was to come.

Her eldest daughter was seriously injured in a road accident at the age of 23. Angela's faith sustained her throughout the duration of this tragedy and gave her the resilience to dedicate the next twenty years to nursing her until she died. Following this immense loss came the arrival of an unexpected spiritual dimension into her life.

'One day, shortly after her funeral, I was in the sitting room, not thinking about her, and I just looked up. There she was, floating in mid-air, her face so sweet and happy, just as she was before she was hurt, smiling and joyful. I could not look too long the first time. The second and third time I was reluctant to look as she was too radiant for me.' Angela worked as a Volunteer in Crumlin Children's Hospital for 26 years, a role which helped provide comfort following her bereavement.

Easy Pavlova

By Nesta Nolan

A simple dessert that always delights. This recipe can be combined with our 21st Century Bread and Butter Pudding to use the egg yolks!

Preparation time 7 minutes *Cooking time* 2 hours *Equipment* Large baking tray, lined with parchment paper *Serves* 6-8

Ingredients

250g/8oz caster sugar
4 large egg whites
1 teaspoon cornflour
1 teaspoon white wine vinegar

Topping
250ml/½ pint fresh cream, whipped
250g/8oz fresh fruit in season

Method

1. Preheat the oven to 150C/300F/Gas mark 2.

2. Whisk the egg whites until stiff then add the sugar, a tablespoon at a time, whisking continuously.

3. Add the cornflour and vinegar and whisk again.

4. Spread the mixture onto a large baking tray lined with parchment paper in a circular shape.

5. Place in the oven and bake for 60 minutes until firm to the touch.

6. Turn the oven off and leave the meringue inside for 1 hour, with the door ajar.

7. Remove the parchment paper and transfer to a serving plate.

8. When ready to serve, whip the cream to soft peaks and spread on top of the meringue.

9. Arrange the fruit over the top and enjoy every mouthful.

Nesta was a lover of food, friends and life. Although cooking wasn't Nesta's forte she enjoyed nothing more than hosting coffee mornings at home where she and her friends would chat and laugh their way through all kinds of topics, sustained by an array of finger sandwiches and cakes.

Throughout her life, Nesta was a student of learning: art, literature and music were her passions, and in her notebooks she collected quotations and excerpts from a wide range of works, which illuminated and expanded her thoughts.

Her favourite dessert was always Pavlova. If she saw some on display in a café, her eyes would light up but then she'd worry about the calories, and her diet, and often the Pavlova remained uneaten. In the end, however, she got her beloved dessert whenever she wanted it. Her last months were spent in great happiness at Blackrock Hospice, where each morning Isaac the chef would come to visit her. 'Nesta' he'd smile, 'tell me what I can make for you today?' Thrilled at such royal treatment she nearly always replied 'Pavlova, please!' In honour of Brigid Nesta Nolan, this simple recipe for Pavlova is one which she would surely approve of.

Apple Tart

By Peggy McHugh

Try this classic apple tart recipe once and you will remember it forever.

Preparation time 30 minutes *Cooking time* 25-35 minutes
Equipment 20cm/8 inch ovenproof pie dish, greased *Serves* 6

Ingredients

225g/8oz plain flour
125g/4oz butter
150ml/¼ pint cold water (approx)

4 large cooking apples, peeled, cored and sliced
100g/4oz sugar, to sweeten apples

Method

1. Preheat the oven to 200C/400F/Gas mark 6.
2. Place the butter in the freezer for about 15 minutes to harden.
3. Sieve the flour into a bowl. Grate the hard butter into the flour then using a knife, mix the grated butter in well.
4. Add sufficient water and mix to a soft dough with the knife. Knead lightly on a floured surface.
5. Roll out half the pastry to the size of the dish and lay inside.
6. Arrange the apple slices on the pastry, covering the base entirely and sprinkle with the sugar.
7. Roll the remaining pastry out to fit the pie. Dampen the edge of the base with cold water to help the top stick.
8. Lay the top over the pie and press the edges together to form a crust. Cut a cross in the centre to allow steam to escape.
9. Bake in the oven for 25-35 minutes or until the top is a nice light golden brown.

From a young age Peggy McHugh was an entrepreneur. Early in their marriage she and her husband Cyril set up a grocery shop called the School Stores. Ever the savvy businesswoman she knew getting customers in was the first challenge so she got a neon Players Wills cigarette sign for the shop to attract customers. Once in the door she was able to sell them anything and everything, with just a little chat and charm.

It wasn't just in business that Peggy used her confidence to her advantage. One evening she was stopped by a Guard and issued a summons for riding a bike without realising it had no lights. She took the punishment, but not lying down! She 'dressed to kill' for court that day and defended herself.

No matter what happened in her life Peggy always felt emboldened by the support of her husband. Years later, this support enabled her to stand up for their son, Oliver, when he had his exam marks unfairly downgraded. Ever the fighter, taking her hat, coat, bag and basket, Peggy marched off to UCD to confront the Professor. The matter was swiftly dealt with and Oliver went on to happily continue his studies in Medicine.

Fig Pudding

By James Fox

This is a sweet and unusual alternative to traditional puddings.

Preparation time 5 minutes *Cooking time* 80-90 minutes
Equipment 2 pint pudding bowl, greased *Serves* 6-8

Ingredients

110g/4oz figs	110/4oz caster sugar
110g/4oz flour	Pinch of salt
110g/4oz breadcrumbs	2 eggs, beaten
1 teaspoon baking powder	1 teaspoon treacle
110g/4oz suet	50ml/3 tablespoons milk

Method

1. Cut the figs into small pieces.

2. Mix the flour, breadcrumbs, baking powder, suet, caster sugar and salt together.

3. Add the beaten eggs, treacle and milk to form a dropping consistency.

4. Pour the pudding mixture into the prepared pudding bowl and cover the top with greaseproof paper.

5. Cover over this again with tin foil and tie with twine around the rim and then over the top to form a handle.

6. Place on an upturned saucer in a saucepan with boiling water coming half-way up the side of the bowl and steam for 80-90 minutes.

7. Turn out onto a plate and serve with custard or cream.

There is a word Jim mentions that he is very fond of, a word that encompasses the virtues that guide him daily. It is the old Irish word 'ráméis', derived from the Norman word for romance. Within this concept lies a profound value for him, one that comprises comfort, healing, consolation and the daily happiness of an enjoyable conversation. A contented life indeed.

Chapter 6

Cakes

Lemon Drizzle Cake

By Susan Huszar

This sticky, lemony cake is a truly tangy delight.

Preparation time 10 minutes *Cooking time* 30-35 minutes
Equipment 2lb loaf tin *Makes* 12 slices

Ingredients

125g/5oz plain flour
125g/5oz butter, softened
125g/5oz caster sugar
2 large eggs
Rind and juice of 1 lemon

Topping:
Grated rind and juice of 1 lemon
2 tablespoons icing sugar

Method

1. Preheat the oven to 180C/350F/Gas mark 4.

2. Mix all the cake ingredients together until smooth and creamy.

3. Pour the batter into a loaf tin and smooth the top with a spoon.

4. Bake in the preheated oven for 30-35 minutes.

5. Mix together the lemon juice, rind, and icing sugar to make the topping.

6. When the cake is cooked leave it in the tin and prick it all over the top with a skewer.

7. Pour the lemon mixture over the hot cake to form a lovely crisp topping.

For Susan, being in the Community Reablement Unit is like a holiday. As the parents and carers of a disabled daughter who doesn't sleep well, an uninterrupted night's sleep is bliss for Susan and her husband. She talks of the atmosphere in the unit as optimistic and shares how the encouraging positivity she encounters there helps to 'reboot' her. Here, too, she gets help and motivation for her own physiotherapy which keeps her supple and flexible, a must for her busy life.

When asked what makes her happy, Susan lists things she already has present in her life. There is a lesson in contentedness here for us all. Showing affection and concern for her family, friends, and the people she meets along life's way are what drive her.

When it comes to coping with difficulties, her motto is simple: 'keep on keeping on.' Her mother brought her up to be polite and considerate and she says these qualities help her to be patient as a carer. Susan has an unfailing ability to see the good in others. From her lifetime of experience she says the one consistent lesson she has learned is; 'a good temper, a sense of humour, and seeing the funny side of life turns reversals of fortune and disappointments into sunshine.'

Guinness Cake

By Etty (Ethel) Murphy

There are as many porter and Guinness Cake recipes as there are Dublin cooks. We are lucky to have two in our current edition. Try both for research purposes!

Preparation time 10 minutes, plus overnight
Cooking time 75-80 minutes *Equipment* 2 x 2lb loaf tins, greased and lined with parchment paper *Makes* 2 lots of 12 slices

Ingredients

450g/1lb sultanas	150g/5oz dark brown sugar
450g/1lb raisins	110g/4oz mixed nuts, chopped
500ml/1 pint Guinness	450g/1lb self-raising flour
3 eggs, beaten	

Method

1. Place the sultanas and raisins in a large bowl and pour over the Guinness. Leave them to steep overnight.

2. The next day, preheat the oven to 160C/320F/Gas mark 3.

3. Add the beaten eggs, the brown sugar and the nuts to the sultana and Guinness combination and mix well.

4. Slowly add the flour and mix well.

5. Pour the mixture into the loaf tins and smooth the tops over with a knife.

6. Bake in the preheated oven for 75-80 minutes or until a skewer inserted into the cakes comes out clean.

7. Cool on a wire rack and leave for at least 24 hours before cutting.

Ethel's mother gave her one sage piece of advice for her married life; 'face life as it comes and get on with whatever it throws at you.'

'Well,' as Ethel, laughingly says, 'like everybody else, life threw bills at me!' As a busy but happy mother of six, Ethel decided she would laugh and bake her way to the bank and embarked on a catering business that utilised her very best talents.

She would get up a 5:45am every morning to prepare her ingredients for the day's orders. A typical morning's baking would often consist of two dozen scones, cream cakes, apple tarts, mince pies and Oxford lunches. The minute she got to the kitchen the oven was turned on, ready for a day of hard work.

For 21st parties, friends always ordered her famous Black Forest Gateaux. It took three days to make as the cherries and chocolate had to be soaked in bowls of Kirsch but Ethel did nothing by halves.

By the time babies five and six arrived, Ethel packed in the catering business and started a new business. No stranger to discipline she embarked on learning a new set of skills, this time the violin, piano and Irish dancing and opened an Irish dancing school. She sums up her passion and vigour for life, 'what was the energy and soul of my youth became the salvation of my life' and tells everyone she meets to 'go to CRU (Community Reablement Unit at Our Lady's Hospice) if you want to feel marvellous again!'

Traditional Porter Cake

By Nuala Duggan

You can time-travel with a porter cake, it takes you right back to your childhood.

Preparation time 15 minutes *Cooking time* 80-90 minutes
Equipment 21cm/8 inch square tin, lined with parchment paper
Makes 20 slices

Ingredients

225g/8oz butter	2 teaspoons mixed spice
225g/8oz sugar	¼ teaspoon bread soda
250ml/½ pint porter	100g/4oz chopped walnuts
565g/20oz mixed sultanas and raisins (or mixed dried fruit)	3 large eggs, beaten
475g/18oz self-raising flour	1 tablespoon marmalade (optional)

Method

1. Preheat the oven to 160C/320F/Gas mark 3.

2. Melt the butter and sugar together in a large saucepan.

3. Add the porter and fruit and bring to the boil before allowing to cool.

4. Add the sieved flour, mixed spice, bread soda, walnuts, beaten eggs and marmalade, if using.

5. Mix well and then pour the mixture into the lined tin and bake for 1 hour and 25 minutes.

6. Remove from the oven and leave in the tin to cool.

7. This cake is delicious spread with thick, real butter and tastes better every day. It will stay fresh in an airtight tin for months.

Nuala was born in 1937 in Drumshambo, famous for Gunpowder Gin and Laird's Jam. In her childhood she saw the pony-led barges towing coal down the Royal Canal essential for Dublin during WWII.

She came from a family that always enjoyed company and fondly remembers the large kitchen table at the heart of her home that could accommodate up to 20 people in a sitting, a place of happy meals, fond friends, close family and the odd spontaneous poker game.

As a young woman Nuala worked as what was known then as a 'hello girl' at the Telecom Exchange on Exchequer Street in Dublin. She met her husband William at a ballroom dance and immediately liked his sense of humour. They had a slow and romantic courtship and went on to have six children.

Nuala's daughter Ann recently died in the Hospice. Nuala's journey through grief is an ongoing one. She deals with it by reminding herself that 'life is short and to enjoy the time you have.' She reminds herself that there are 7 billion people in the world, 'don't let one tragedy ruin your life.'

Nevertheless, it is still a very difficult journey and her passage through it is eased by occasionally lighting a candle to burn her cares away. Singing helps her too. Nuala belongs to Memory Lane Choir, and enjoys singing songs she learned as a child. Now, she says, she values 'contentment, blessed normality, and the generosity of my family and friends.'

Pineapple Upside-Down Cake

By Maura O'Sullivan

This is one of the easiest, hassle-free desserts that Maura has ever made. Kids like it because it looks novel and adults think it is retro because it brings back memories of 70s dishes like Prawn Cocktail and Baked Alaska. Many of her friends have acquired this recipe from her to create their own nostalgia.

Preparation time 30 minutes *Cooking time* 30-35 minutes
Equipment 18cm/7 inch fixed-bottomed cake tin, greased *Serves* 6-8

Ingredients

2 tablespoons sugar
6 slices tinned pineapple, in juice
75g/3oz glacé cherries
100g/4oz plain flour
1 teaspoon baking powder

¼ teaspoon bread soda
100g/4oz butter, at room temperature
100g/4oz caster sugar
2 large eggs

3 tablespoons pineapple juice from the fruit
Fresh cream or ice cream to serve

Method

1. Preheat the oven to 200C/400F/Gas mark 6.

2. Sprinkle the two tablespoons of sugar onto the base of the greased tin.

3. Arrange the pineapple slices in a circle around the base with one in the centre.

4. Place a cherry in the centre of each slice and then more around the centre slice.

5. Put the flour, baking powder, bread soda, butter, sugar and eggs in a food processor and process until the batter is smooth.

6. Add the pineapple juice to thin the mixture a little.

7. Pour the batter carefully over the pineapple rings and spread gently to cover.

8. Bake in the preheated oven for 30-35 minutes.

9. Insert a palette knife carefully around the edge of the tin to ease away the cake.

10. Place a plate on top of the tin and turn the cake over onto it.

11. Allow to cool and serve with fresh cream or ice cream.

Hollywood Cake
By Maeve Cahalane

Maeve's mother, Noreen, was always happy baking in her kitchen in Ballyluskey, and this was one of her favourite recipes, which delighted all 12 of the family! There's no baking required so it's a really easy way to make a yummy treat.

Preparation time 15 minutes *Chilling time:* 24 hours
Equipment 20cm/8 inch square cake tin *Makes* 20 squares

Ingredients

100g/4oz butter
100g/4oz sugar
1 large egg, beaten

2 tablespoons cocoa
or drinking chocolate

225g/8oz Rich Tea or
similar biscuits

Method

1. In a bowl over a pot of boiling water, melt the butter and sugar together gently.

2. Mix in the cocoa or drinking chocolate powder.

3. Stir in the beaten egg and simmer gently for 3 minutes, stirring all the time.

4. Put the biscuits into a plastic bag and use a rolling pin to crush them.

5. Stir the crushed biscuits and then pour the entire mixture into the tin, pressing it down firmly.

6. Leave to set in the fridge for 24 hours.

7. Cut into squares and store in an airtight tin or box.

Raspberry and Amaretti Crunch Cake

By Emer Sheridan

This unique cake combines so many delicious flavours and textures. The soft buttery sponge is contrasted by the crunchy Ameretti buscuits and the sweetness is cut through with the tart oozing taste of fresh raspberries. This really is a dessert with a difference!

Preparation time 15 minutes *Cooking time* 50-55 minutes
Equipment 20cm/8 inch round, loose-bottomed cake tin, greased and lined *Serves* 6-8

Ingredients

175g/6oz butter, at room temperature	140g/5oz self-raising flour	250g/8oz punnet raspberries
175g/6oz golden caster sugar	85g/2oz ground almonds	1 tablespoon icing sugar, to decorate
3 large eggs	140g/5oz Amaretti biscuits – roughly broken	

Method

1. Preheat the oven to 160C/325F/Gas mark 3.

2. Put the butter, caster sugar, eggs, flour and ground almonds into a large bowl, and beat together until well blended.

3. Spread half the cake mixture into the lined tin and scatter half the Amaretti biscuits on top.

4. Take around 100g/3oz of the raspberries and press very lightly into the top of the cake mixture.

5. Drop the remaining cake mixture in spoonfuls over the Amaretti and raspberries, and spread evenly.

6. Scatter the remaining Amaretti biscuits and 100g/3oz more of the raspberries over the top.

7. Bake for 50-55 mins, until a skewer inserted into the centre comes out clean.

8. Cool for 15 minutes in the tin then run a knife round the edge and turn out.

9. Refrigerate until required.

10. Remove from the fridge an hour before serving and lightly dust the top with the icing sugar.

11. Serve with cream or custard, and sprinkle the remaining raspberries on top.

12. This cake will keep in a covered container in the fridge for up to 2 days.

Walnut Coffee Cake

By Alice Victory

This cake pretty much covers any possible dining eventuality; delicious for a coffee morning, perfect for afternoon tea, or enjoy with whipped cream for dessert.

Preparation time 10 minutes *Cooking time* 20-25 minutes
Equipment 24 x 34cm/9 x 13 inch Swiss roll tin *Serves* 10-12

Ingredients

300g/11oz self-raising flour

1 level teaspoon baking powder

225g/8oz soft butter

225g/8oz caster sugar

4 large eggs

3 teaspoons instant coffee dissolved in

2 tablespoons hot water

100g/4oz chopped walnuts

Icing:

50g/2oz butter, melted

2 teaspoons instant coffee dissolved in,

2 tablespoons hot water

225g/8oz icing sugar

Walnut halves for decoration

Method

1. Preheat the oven to 180C/350F/Gas mark 4.

2. Line the tin with baking parchment.

3. Place all the cake ingredients into a mixing bowl and beat thoroughly for around 3 minutes until smooth and creamy.

4. Transfer the cake mixture to the tin and spread evenly. Smooth over the top.

5. Bake for 25-30 minutes until firm to the touch in the middle.

6. Remove from the tin and cool on a wire rack.

7. Make the icing by beating all the ingredients together then allow to cool.

8. When the cake is completely cold, spread the icing over the top generously with a palette knife.

9. Cut into squares and place a walnut half on each square.

When it comes to the usual highs and lows of life, Alice has had more than her fair share.

The highs were high indeed. She met her husband Michael while he was courting her friend; she was the 'go-between' until he realized it was Alice he truly loved. On her 21st Birthday, he asked her to marry him but she turned him down. That was a Thursday. By the Friday she had changed her mind. They lived happily together with their children: Ruth, Jean, Eric, Eileen and David. She has also been lucky in other ways, she has won money on Winning Streak, not just once but twice. However, nothing could have prepared her for the deepest low she would ever experience in her life.

Two years ago, her son Eric committed suicide, aged just 46. His son, her grandson, was just seven years old. Eric was a very intelligent man. Though he entered academic life he didn't take to it and instead he became a craft carpenter. He was a genius with his hands and a magician with wood. Alice remembers that as a young boy Eric designed and built a periscope so he could see the Pope during his 1979 visit. It was so successful that he hardly got a chance to look through it, everyone else wanted a view. That was her clever, bright boy. Alice will never forget the day he left for the USA, for just a holiday she thought. He said to her, 'Ma, have you a bigger suitcase?' She asked why and he replied 'because I'm staying.'

Lemon Butter Cake

By John and Úna Fletcher

Úna has made this cake for 62 years since she first saw it in Woman's Weekly. It is always unfailingly welcomed by her seven grandchildren and their friends.

Preparation time 10 minutes *Cooking time* 20 minutes hours
Equipment 23 x 30cm/9 x 12 inch Swiss roll tin *Makes* 30 squares

---

Ingredients

175g/6oz sugar	Grated rind and juice of 2 lemons
175g/6oz butter	
175g/6oz self-raising flour	175g/6oz sugar (for the drizzle topping)
2 eggs	

Method

1. Preheat the oven to 180C/350F/Gas mark 4.

2. Place the sugar, butter, flour, eggs, and lemon rind into a bowl. Beat together for about 2 minutes until smooth and creamy.

3. Spread the mixture into the tin and smooth the top over with a knife.

4. Place in the preheated oven for 20 minutes.

5. While cooking, mix the lemon juice and sugar together for the drizzle.

6. When the cake is cooked and still hot, pour this mixture over the top.

7. Allow to cool, then cut into squares and enjoy.

Úna and John have been happily married for 57 years. John is one of ten children. His family were devoted to hurling and camogie and John was a regular in Croke Park to watch his sister play in the Inter-County games. It wasn't long before he was cheering Úna on as well. They used to meet at Céilís around town and by the time that they were married, several years later, they were already completely devoted to each other. Though the infamous marriage bar meant that Úna had to leave her job, she soon found that work inside the home was just as challenging as work outside.

They bought their little red-brick house off the plans and soon settled into a small and caring community. It was the perfect place to raise a family; neighbours looked after each other and mothers would wheel their babies out together daily. The house had a coal-fired boiler which required constant vigilance. In the back yard, nappies hung like flags across the line, fluttering with the breeze. Later on, the first Hoover washing machine arrived: a tub and paddle on one side, and a spindle with a wire basket for squeezing the water out on the other – total luxury.

Life was about work and family, the two inextricably intertwined but never begrudged. Úna's day revolved around John and their three children. She says even now that she was always happy, never worried. They credit the happiness and longevity of their marriage to two simple things: they saw each other's point of view and they never fought, only argued. Úna was the peacemaker and John, as Úna puts it, 'was wonderful!'

Cherry Cake

By James Fox

This recipe is taken from a recipe book written by Jim's mother which is dated January 1930, and from which he acquires all his favourite recipes.

Preparation time 10 minutes *Cooking time* 60-65 minutes
Equipment 20cm/8 inch round cake tin, lined with parchment
Serves 6-8

Ingredients

225g/8oz butter
225g/8oz caster sugar
1 teaspoon baking powder
450g/1lb flour
4 eggs, beaten until frothy
225g/8oz glacé cherries, halved
50ml/3 tablespoons whiskey

Method

1. Preheat the oven to 180C/360F/Gas mark 4.

2. Beat the butter and sugar together until they form a creamy consistency.

3. Stir the baking powder into the flour.

4. Add the flour and beaten eggs alternately, beating the mixture well between additions.

5. Stir in the cherries and whiskey and stir through one final time.

6. Pour the mixture into the prepared tin and bake for 60-65 minutes, until golden and firm to the touch.

7. Allow to cool before removing from the tin.

Born the eldest of seven siblings, in 1947, aged just 8, Jim and his family moved from his mother's family home to his father's dairy farm. With the furniture transported on the back of the tractor, the family, their cows and other animals walked the seven miles to their new home.

Food was life on the farm and the family sold the best of the produce and ate the rest. Everything was used, nothing was wasted. Meat was home cured (the bacon hung in the chimney) and chickens and turkeys were truly free-range. Flour bags were made of calico, you sewed two together to make a bed-sheet. The farm produced hay and grew corn and maize, ground oats and beets. Turnips, potatoes, carrots, parsnips, cabbages and onions were stored in pits in the fields.

Jim was an altar boy in the local church from a young age. It was tempting for parents back then to prize security and stability and encourage their sons to join the priesthood. Jim's parents resisted and instead Jim won a scholarship for secondary school and went on to Agricultural College at UCC.

Now retired, following a lifetime of hard work, Jim only does the things he wants to do. He gives history lectures for Men's Sheds and is a guide in the Pearse Museum in Rathfarnham. Where once it was hard work and commitment, the virtues Jim prizes now are thoughtfulness, resilience of spirit, and looking to the future.

BAKERY
FLOUR

Toblerone Cheese Cake

By Aileen Keane

There are probably hundreds of different cheesecake recipes out there but this one is a really special one. If you love Toblerone then you'll happily devour more than one slice of this rich and decadent dessert. If you don't love Toblerone, swap it for any other chocolate bar you enjoy and you'll have a brand new recipe!

Preparation time 15 minutes *Cooking time* 3 hours or overnight
Equipment 18cm/7 inch loose-bottomed tin, lightly greased *Serves* 12

Ingredients

150g/5oz digestive biscuits, crumbed

50g/2oz butter, melted

280g/10oz light cream cheese

180g/6oz Toblerone milk chocolate, melted

20g/1oz Toblerone milk chocolate, grated

250ml/½ pint fresh cream, lightly whipped

Method

1. Combine the biscuit crumbs and the melted butter together in a bowl.

2. Press the mixture firmly down into the base of the tin and place in the fridge to chill.

3. Beat the cheese until smooth, then fold in the whipped cream and the melted chocolate until well combined.

4. Pour the cheesecake mix onto the chilled biscuit base, and return to the fridge for 3 hours or overnight.

5. Sprinkle the top with the grated chocolate and devour!

Hazelnut Meringue Cake with Melba Sauce

By Grace Murray

Delicious as a dessert or for a summer afternoon tea party.

Preparation time 30 minutes *Cooking time* 30-40 minutes
Equipment 2 x 20cm/8 inch sandwich tins *Serves* 6-8

Ingredients

Meringue:
4 large egg whites
255g/9oz caster sugar
3-4 drops vanilla essence
½ teaspoon vinegar
100g/4oz hazelnuts, ground and toasted
Icing sugar for dusting

Filling:
250ml/½ pint double cream
225g/8oz raspberries
1 tablespoon icing sugar
Vanilla essence
Melba Sauce:
225g/8oz fresh or frozen raspberries
4 tablespoons icing sugar, sifted

Method

1. Preheat the oven to 190C/375F/Gas mark 5.
2. Butter and flour the sides of the tins and line the bases.
3. Whisk the egg whites until stiff. Then add the sugar, a tablespoon at a time, beating until it is stiff and stands in peaks.
4. Whisk in the vanilla essence and vinegar, then fold in the hazelnuts.
5. Divide the mixture between the tins and bake for 30-40 minutes but no longer. Turn onto wire racks to cool.
6. Whisk the cream until thick then whisk in the icing sugar and vanilla essence.
7. Purée the fresh or frozen (but defrosted) raspberries and sieve them, then beat in the sifted icing sugar, one tablespoon at a time.
8. Cover one of the meringues with the cream and fresh raspberries, place the other on top and dust with icing sugar.
9. You can serve the sauce on the side or drizzle over the top of the meringue.

Grace's daughters remember their mum telling them how shortly after she married their father he told her, tongue-firmly-in-cheek, how she'd better learn to cook!

Never one to back down from a challenge she enrolled in the first of, what turned out to be many, cooking classes. From this sprang a lifelong love of food and cooking.

Grace became legendary for her newly acquired skills and Sundays always saw a few 'unexpected visitors' drop around on the off-chance of some leftovers going a-begging. The girls laugh as they recall their friends, some from as far as five miles away, calling and saying 'oh I just happened to be passing by...' but Grace was always happy to share and entertaining was a great love of hers.

As her children grew older Grace turned once more to pursuing her own interests again and cooking was chief among them. She spent many wonderful weekends away at the Ballymaloe Cookery School but thankfully never stopped cooking for her precious family.

Pineapple Roll

By Carmel Hennessy

This is such a quick and easy dessert and can be made minutes before guests arrive

---

Preparation time 15 minutes *Cooking time* 10 minutes
Equipment 23 x 31cm/9 x 13 inch Swiss roll tin *Serves* 4-6

Ingredients

4 eggs

125g/4oz sugar

175g/6oz self-raising flour

Fresh pineapple (tinned is fine)

250ml/½ pint fresh cream

Method

1. Preheat the oven to 200C/400F/Gas mark 6.

2. Line the tin with parchment paper.

3. Beat the eggs and sugar together until creamy and thick, so that the beater leaves a trail in the mixture.

4. Fold in the flour gently and gradually, taking care not to leave any white lumps.

5. Pour into the tin and bake in the oven for 7-8 minutes until the sponge is golden and firm to the touch.

6. Turn onto the greaseproof paper and trim the sides.

7. Roll up like a Swiss roll and then allow to cool.

8. Whip the fresh cream and crush the pineapple and mix together.

9. Unroll the sponge and spread with the pineapple mixture, roll it back up again and serve with whipped cream.

Carmel's mother owned The Pavilion Hotel in Dun Laoghaire, and, a natural caterer, she ran it beautifully. Inspired by this, Carmel followed her mother into the same field; she worked as a cook for nineteen years in the canteen for staff in Jacobs. She loved her colleagues and particularly loved the highlight of the year for the team, catering for the Jacob's TV Awards annual ceremony. This event often entailed catering for up to 800 people. With a full complement of kitchen staff, the busy and happy team would start early and finish late. Once they cooked eighteen salmon for one dinner!

When her mother fell ill, Carmel nursed her at home until she was 38, and then she was cared for in the Hospice for thirteen months where she was so well looked after that she was able to come home for what turned out to be her final six months. Carmel is a huge supporter of the work of the Hospice. For eighteen years she participated with the Browne and Gleeson families in their 100-year fundraising endeavour for Sr Francis Rose and the Hospice. She was seventy- and eighty-years old, still driving around every second Sunday collecting envelopes from Milltown, Dundrum and Donnybrook. Her collection book used to be placed on the altar in honour of this wonderful work, and it is now in the Hospice Museum among the memorabilia. Now in her nineties Carmel has taken up painting landscapes and flowers and plans on leaving all her paintings to the Hospice.

Dutch Spiced Apple Cake

By Angela Curran

The addition of spices makes this apple cake stand out from the crowd. It's very quick to prepare and though surprisingly simple, it is utterly gorgeous.

Preparation time 30 minutes *Cooking time* 30-40 minutes
Equipment 2 x 20cm/8 inch sandwich tins *Serves* 6-8

Ingredients

150g/6oz shortcrust pastry, ready made
900g/2lb cooking apples, thinly sliced
110g/4oz brown sugar

1 teaspoon cinnamon
¼ teaspoon grated nutmeg
90g/3oz chopped almonds
60g/2oz butter for topping

Method

1. Preheat the oven to 200C/400F/Gas mark 6.

2. Roll out the pastry thinly, then line the tin with it and crimp the edges neatly.

3. Cover the pastry with overlapping slices of apple.

4. Mix together the brown sugar and the spices and chopped nuts, and sprinkle the mixture over the apples.

5. Dot shavings of butter over the apple slices.

6. Bake for 30-40 mins until the pastry and the apples are cooked through.

7. Leave to cool, then cut into fingers or squares and serve.

My five Irish children and my twelve grandchildren adore this Apple Cake. The secret is to add nuts, not just almonds, but chopped Brazil nuts, hazelnuts, walnuts, whatever is in your storehouse. Be careful, though, to warn guests and visitors who might have a nut allergy, to abstain – the best idea is to have two Apple Cakes, one with more spices and no nuts, so there is a choice, both will disappear with delighted cries of 'Is there any more?'

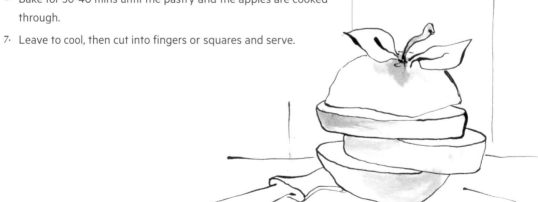

Chapter 7

Home Baking

Hollie and Katie's Flapjacks
By Angela Kavanagh

Angela's teenage daughter, Hollie, does all the baking in their house at the moment and while Angela's older daughter, Katie, lays claim to the provenance of this recipe, it is nonetheless a family favourite.

Preparation time 10 minutes *Cooking time* 10-15 minutes
Equipment 18 x 28cm/7 x 11 inch Swiss roll tin *Makes* 25 squares or 30 fingers

Ingredients
150g/6oz butter   225g/8oz oats
150g/6oz brown sugar   Pinch of salt

Method
1. Preheat the oven to 180C/350F/Gas mark 4.
2. Line the baking tin with parchment paper.
3. Melt the butter in a medium-sized saucepan.
4. Add the sugar, oats, and salt, and stir well.
5. Pour into the prepared tin and press down to make an even surface.
6. Bake in the preheated oven for 10-15 minutes until golden brown.
7. Cool in the tray and then cut into fingers or squares, as desired.

Tea Brack

By Trevor Creevey

Trevor's mother always uses this recipe, which was passed to her in turn from her mother. Many of Trevor's friends have also acquired the recipe, having tasted the results in his house!

Preparation time 5 minutes plus overnight *Cooking time* 90-95 minutes
Equipment 2 x 20cm/8 inch round tins, or 2 x 2lb loaf tins *Makes* 2 x 12 slices

Ingredients

420ml/¾ pint cold tea	2 large eggs	1 teaspoon ginger
675g/1½ lb mixed dried fruit	375g/14oz self-raising flour	
275g/10oz dark brown sugar	2 teaspoons mixed spice	

Method

1. Place the cold tea, fruit, and sugar in a large bowl and steep overnight.

2. Next day, preheat the oven to 180C/350F/Gas mark 4.

3. Add the rest of the ingredients to the tea mixture and mix well.

4. Divide the mixture evenly into the two round or loaf tins.

5. Bake in the preheated oven for 90-95 minutes until the top feels firm to the touch.

6. Cover the top of the cake with brown paper if it is in danger of becoming burned.

Banana Bread

By Joanna McNamara

Joanna's banana bread is a simple, tasty recipe that can and should be enjoyed as a pleasure all of its own.

Preparation time 10 minutes *Cooking time* 50-55 minutes
Equipment 2lb loaf tin, greased and lined with parchment paper
Makes 12 slices

Ingredients

125g/4oz butter	1 teaspoon cinnamon
125g/4oz light brown sugar	1 teaspoon vanilla essence
2 large free-range eggs	250g/8oz self-raising flour
2 large bananas, mashed	100g/4oz walnuts, chopped

Method

1. Preheat the oven to 160C/325F/Gas mark 3.

2. Put the butter, sugar, eggs, mashed banana, cinnamon, and vanilla essence into a bowl and beat well.

3. Add the flour and stir into the mixture.

4. Remove about 2 tablespoons of chopped walnuts for decoration and mix the remainder into the banana bread mixture.

5. Transfer to the prepared tin, scatter the reserved walnuts on top, and bake for about 50 minutes until well-risen and a knife gently pressed into the bread comes out clean.

6. Allow to rest in the tin for about 10 minutes then turn onto a wire tray to cool.

7. When cold wrap in greaseproof paper and tinfoil to keep fresh.

Joanna McNamara is a 34 year-old Polish woman married to a 'very loving and supportive' Irish academic named Cormac. Despite her young age, Joanna attends the rheumatology clinic regularly and is delighted to be in its care. She benefits from the in-patient pain management programme; something that has not just helped her manage pain but to learn how to cope with the challenges of her condition. This group has helped her gain confidence in herself, her abilities and the possibilities ahead for her. Being a patient in Our Lady's has taken a lot of the fear away from her daily life and that has been crucial for her.

For many people happiness is a state of being, for Joanna it is a state of mind and to be found in the small moments she can enjoy in her life. She devours books on history, politics, art and philosophy and considers reading outdoor in the sunshine one of the simpler pleasures in her life. Happiness can also be found in the pursuit of creative pastimes; painting, dressmaking and embroidery: the act of creation leaving a lasting sense of contentment. Finally, for Joanna, happiness is found in her private and strong relationship with God and her own unique place in the world amongst family and friends.

Fig and Date Bread

By Peter Corrigan

This is a lovely, moist, sweet-tasting bread and ideal for breakfast or as a mid-morning snack.

Preparation time 20 minutes (plus 2 hours to rise) *Cooking time* 30-35 minutes *Equipment* Baking tray, lined with parchment paper *Makes* 2 small round loaves

Ingredients

400g/14oz wholemeal flour
100g/4oz strong white flour, plus extra for dusting
1 teaspoon salt
20g/1oz yeast

50g/2oz butter, softened
1 tablespoon treacle
300ml/½ pint warm water
75g/3oz figs, chopped
75g/3oz dates, chopped

Method

1. Put the flours, salt, yeast, butter, treacle and water into a bowl and mix by hand for around 5 minutes.

2. Tip out the dough onto a lightly floured surface and knead for 5 minutes.

3. Mix the figs and dates into the dough and knead for a further 5 minutes.

4. Put the dough back into the bowl, cover with a cloth, and leave for 1 hour to rise.

5. Divide the dough in half and shape each half into a ball.

6. Place on a lined baking tray and leave to rise for 1 hour.

7. Meanwhile, preheat the oven to 220C/425F/Gas mark 7.

8. Dust the risen loaves with flour and, using a knife, make three cuts across the top of each loaf.

9. Bake for 30-35 minutes until the loaf sounds hollow when tapped.

10. Place on a wire rack to cool.

When asked what happiness means to him, Peter's answer is simple, unexpected and charming: 'Happiness is building, happiness is cooking, and happiness is family,' he says.

All three of these qualities came together naturally in his life. Thanks to his experience as a builder, he created his dream home for his family in Wicklow from salvage; every stone, beam and window, lovingly placed by his own hands. When he had to sell this because of the financial crash it broke his heart. Not put off however, he went on to transform a shed in the back garden of the house he shares with his son. Now he has a beautiful independent stone cottage with its own entrance from the back lane. He is planning to construct a painted glass window which he will make from small pieces of glass he will seal together, 'sort of like stained glass, but not really, more like art in glass.' Mondrian is his muse. He would like to copy his geometric patterns but include his own vision and colour arrangement into the piece.

He talks of his cooking with the same passion he exhibits for building and creating. 'Happiness is baking bread!' Peter says smiling. 'When my son was going to Italy to meet his girlfriend's parents I made a loaf of my Fig and Date Bread for him to take over and they asked for the recipe' he explains. 'Imagine,' he exclaims with delight, 'my bread baked in Italy!'

Granny's Oat Cakes

By Catherine O'Donoghue

This is a family recipe that has been passed on from Catherine's grandmother, Granny McGlinchy. Numerous family members have baked the recipe over the years, with varying degrees of success. This is Catherine's personal adaptation and she believes it to be the ultimate one!

Preparation time 25 minutes *Cooking time* 40-45 minutes
Equipment Baking tray, greased and heated in oven *Makes* 40-50

Ingredients

250g/8oz butter
200g/6oz sugar

250g/8oz wheaten meal/
wholemeal flour

500g/1lb plain flour
3 large eggs, beaten

Method

1. Preheat the oven to 140C/275F/Gas mark 1.

2. Melt the butter in a saucepan over a low heat.

3. Dissolve the sugar in the butter and leave to cool.

4. Mix the flour and wheaten meal together.

5. Add the butter mixture to the dry ingredients and bind the two together with sufficient beaten egg to form a stiff dough.

6. Divide the mixture in two.

7. Roll each piece of dough out to approximately 1cm/½ inch thickness.

8. Cut into squares and place the squares on the heated, greased baking tray and bake for 40-45 minutes.

9. Place on a wire rack to cool.

10. These can be eaten with butter and jam or marmalade, or are equally delicious with butter and cheese.

Chocolate Eclairs
By Mary Gannon

Mary remembers 'a lovely smell of baking from my next door neighbour Teresa Behan'. This is one of Teresa's recipes and Mary is delighted to share it.

Preparation time 30 minutes *Cooking time* 30-35 minutes
Equipment 23 X 36cm/9 X 14 inch baking tray, lined with parchment *Makes* 45 eclairs, each 4cm/1½ inch long

Ingredients

Choux Pastry:
65g/2½oz butter
150ml/5½fl oz water
90g/3½ oz plain flour
A pinch of salt
2 large free-range eggs, beaten
Cream Filling:
250ml/½ pint fresh cream

50g/2oz icing sugar
1 teaspoon vanilla essence or
1 tablespoon Bailey's
Icing:
200g/7oz icing sugar
30g/1oz cocoa
1 tablespoon water

Method

1. Preheat the oven to 220C/425F/Gas mark 7.

2. Bring the butter and water to a rolling boil in a saucepan on a high heat. Add the flour and salt and beat with a wooden spoon. Return to the heat for 1 minute, stirring all the time.

3. Allow to cool for 5 minutes before adding the beaten eggs gradually, beating between each addition.

4. Pipe short lines of pastry onto the baking tray and bake in the oven for 10 minutes.

5. Reduce the temperature to 200C/400F/Gas mark 6 and bake for a further 15-20 minutes.

6. Remove from the oven and puncture the side of each éclair with a skewer. Return to the oven for a further 5 minutes then allow to cool for at least 30 minutes.

7. Combine the fresh cream, Bailey's and icing sugar and whip until stiff.

8. Pipe the cream mixture into the eclairs through the hole in the side.

9. Sift the icing ingredients together, add a tablespoon of boiling water and mix, then place a teaspoon of icing on top of each éclair and smooth over.

Mary's life changed forever when she broke her back as a child. It was the most innocent of activities, playing on a swing that led to disastrous injuries. From then on, much of her time was spent in her wheelchair, watching others play outside her hospital window.

Eventually, when she was discharged, she suffered another blow, this time an emotional one for a little girl. She could take none of her toys from the hospital home with her for fear of infection. Too young to understand, she remembers only the heartbreak.

Aged 23 Mary married the love of her life, Eddie. She sadly lost him after 49 happy years but finds great comfort and happiness when her grandchildren visit for their regular cooking lessons. 'Are you making the cakes today?'" they ask, and the answer is always 'yes.'

Mary says that her treatment in the Community Reablement Unit is essential to help her manage her condition, the kindness and care she receives there is second to none. Mary's life has, in many ways, resembled that of the heroine of those famous childhood novels *What Katy Did*. Katy swung too high and came a cropper and had to learn to accept her new fate, and she did, in a thoughtful and courageous way.

Chocolate Squares

By Nuala Duggan

Who doesn't enjoy a sticky, crumbly, chocolate brownie? Pair these with a tall glass of cold milk and you have sweet perfection.

Preparation time 10 minutes *Cooking time* 20-30 minutes
Equipment 18 X 28cm/7 X 11 inch Swiss roll tin, lined with parchment paper *Makes* 24 squares

Ingredients

250g/9oz self-raising flour
50g/2oz drinking chocolate powder
¼ teaspoon baking powder
50g/2oz caster sugar

50g/2oz brown sugar
100g/4oz butter
4 eggs
150ml/¼ pint milk

Method

1. Sift the flour, drinking chocolate, and baking powder together into a bowl.

2. Stir in both types of sugar.

3. Melt the butter in the microwave and add to the dry mixture.

4. In a separate bowl, beat the eggs and milk together and add to the mixture, blending thoroughly.

5. Spread the mixture into the tin and bake for 20-30 minutes.

6. Cool on a wire rack, then cut into squares.

Nuala met William Duggan at Clery's Ballroom in August 1960. He was a retired amateur boxer and had represented Ireland in the 1952 Olympics in Helsinki. William was then working at Ford's Dagenham in England and was home on holidays. She liked his sense of humour. Nuala's job enabled her to make long distance calls and they got to know each very well. At Halloween, he proposed under the light of the silvery moon and they married on the 3rd April 1961. They moved to England, where Philip and the twins, Catherine and Anne, were born. Hilary, William, and PJ were born in Dublin. The Duggans and the Mullins are both large families and you never knew who might call in unexpectedly. Having chocolate squares in a tin in a press was always very handy.

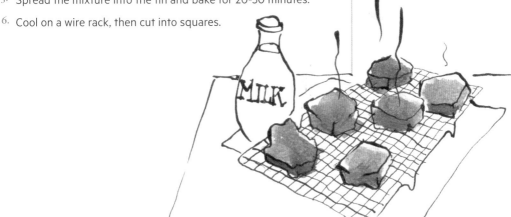

Aunt Maggie's Brown Bread

By Mary Shortt

Mary's good advice to 'eat your porridge and brown bread' is encapsulated in this fine, traditional recipe.

Preparation time 15 minutes *Cooking time* 45-50 minutes
Equipment A deep 20cm/8 inch round tin or a 2lb loaf tin
Makes 12 slices

Ingredients

225g/½lb plain flour
1½ teaspoon salt
454g/1lb coarse wholemeal flour
40g/1½oz wheatgerm

50g/2oz butter
1 teaspoon baking powder
1 teaspoon bread soda
425ml/¾ pint buttermilk

Method

1. Preheat the oven to 200C/400F/Gas mark 6.

2. Brush the tin with melted butter and dust with a little bit of the wholemeal flour.

3. Sieve the plain flour, baking powder, bread soda and salt into a bowl and stir in the wholemeal flour and wheatgerm.

4. Rub in the butter until the mixture resembles breadcrumbs and mix well.

5. Add the buttermilk and mix to a soft dough. Bring the dough together lightly and turn onto a table or board dusted with wholemeal flour.

6. Knead lightly until smooth and place into the prepared tin. Bake in the preheated oven for 20 minutes.

7. Reduce the temperature to 190C/375F/Gas mark 5 and leave for a further 25 minutes.

8. The bread should sound hollow when tapped. If not, return it to the oven for a short while.

9. Remove from the oven and wrap it in a clean tea-towel as this helps to keep the crust soft.

Mary feels so strongly about how the Hospice has supported her and eased her pain that she calls it a 'heavenly place of healing'. It's not just the physical side of her that has been cared for here. She gets such emotional guidance, encouragement and support that it has had a profound effect on her life.

Mary is certain that, though she has faced huge challenges, her experiences have provided her with strength, courage and tenacity. She has learned that she is in charge of her own life and can stand up for herself and make her own decisions. Adversity truly has made her stronger.

She laughingly says her secret for old age is: 'eat your porridge and brown bread.' However she earnestly advises that as life continues to be full of challenges and adventures, it's up to the individual to be prepared to deal with them. Go into old age prepared, know the challenges you may face and organise to be able to manage them. As much as you can, take charge of your own life.

Recently, she was taken to three hospitals in a row and unhappy with the decisions made said 'I am discharging myself, I am fine.' She did and she was. Finally, she closes with this sage and offbeat last piece of advice: 'don't die before you are dead.'

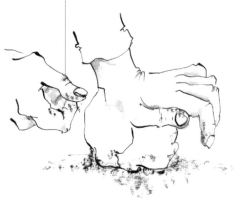

Oatmeal Brown Bread
By Róisín Ryan

This bread is flour-free and fibre-rich and packed full of seeds and healthy grains.

Preparation time 10 minutes *Cooking time* 40-45 minutes
Equipment 2lb loaf tin *Makes* 12 generous slices

Ingredients

500g natural yogurt
420g/14oz porridge oatmeal
1 level teaspoon salt
1 teaspoon bread soda

1 tablespoon each of sesame, poppy, sunflower, pumpkin seeds (or 100g packet mixed seeds)

Method

1. Preheat the oven to 180C/350F/Gas mark 4.

2. Line the tin with parchment paper.

3. Place all the ingredients into a mixing bowl and stir until a thick dough is formed.

4. Pour into the tin and smooth the top over.

5. Bake in the preheated oven for 40-45 minutes until golden brown.

6. Leave in the tin to cool slightly then turn onto a wire rack.

7. This brown bread is delicious served with lashings of butter and jam.

Sit down and make your miserable life happy. These were the forceful yet encouraging words Róisín's mother used to tell her if she ever felt discontented, using them to empower her to create her own happiness. Róisín took the advice and from a young age learned to cope with each day as it arose and how to take charge of the course of her own life.

One fateful day however, took her life on an amazing journey of happiness; the day she met the man of her dreams. When the neighbour's Bed and Breakfast was full-up, by chance Róisín's mother happened to hear and offered to take in a student to stay as a favour to them. A friendship bloomed between Róisín and the student and she fell in love with 'the most wonderful man in the world'. Three children and 54 years of marriage later Róisín is confident she has a beautiful marriage.

Paris Buns

By Sister Imelda

Ask anyone in Northern Ireland or Scotland what Paris Buns are and they'll tell you these sweet, bready cakes were the comforting taste of their childhood. Many a Belfast bakery could testify to their popularity. Funnily enough there is no general consensus on how they got their name but try making them for yourself and you'll see why they are so fondly remembered.

Preparation time 10 minutes *Cooking time* 25-30 minutes
Equipment A baking tray lined with parchment paper *Makes* 10

Ingredients

400g/14oz plain flour
2 teaspoons baking powder
100g/4oz butter

120g/5oz caster sugar
2 large eggs, beaten
120ml/¼ pint milk

Extra milk for brushing on buns
Extra sugar for sprinkling on top

Method

1. Preheat the oven to 190C/375F/Gas mark 5.

2. Sieve the flour and baking powder into a bowl.

3. Finely dice the butter and rub into the flour using the tips of your fingers.

4. Add the sugar and mix thoroughly.

5. Add the beaten egg and milk and stir to form a dough.

6. Roll the dough into 10 evenly-sized balls and place on a baking tray lined with parchment paper.

7. Brush each bun with milk and sprinkle with sugar.

8. Bake in the preheated oven for 25-30 minutes.

9. Eat as they are or with butter and jam.

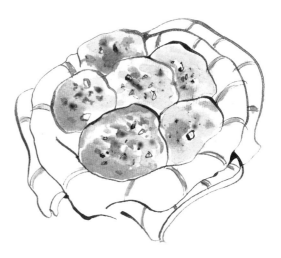

Oaty Banana, Cranberry, & Dark Chocolate Muffins *By Aoife McCormack*

These muffins are really tasty and only take 15 minutes to prepare. Blueberries can also be added as the flavours combine well. They are a lovely afternoon snack with a cup of tea or heated up with some vanilla ice cream for dessert!

Preparation time 10 minutes *Cooking time* 15 minutes
Equipment 12-hole muffin tin, Paper cases to fit *Makes* 12

Ingredients

180g/6½oz plain flour
100g/3½oz porridge oats
75g/3oz caster sugar
2 teaspoons baking powder
½ teaspoon salt

1 egg, beaten lightly
175ml/6fl oz milk
75ml/3fl oz vegetable oil
1 teaspoon vanilla extract
3-4 bananas (roughly 250g),

mashed
50g/2oz dark chocolate, chopped finely
200g/7oz dried cranberries

Method

1. Preheat the oven to 200C/400F/Gas mark 6.

2. Combine the flour, oats, sugar, baking powder and salt in a large mixing bowl.

3. In a separate bowl mix the egg, milk, oil and vanilla.

4. Add the mashed banana to the egg and milk mixture and stir thoroughly.

5. Add the flour mixture and the chocolate and cranberries.

6. Mix all the ingredients thoroughly.

7. Line the muffin tin with cases and divide the batter among them.

8. Bake for 18-20 minutes until golden brown.

9. Place on a wire rack to cool.

Rhubarb Bread

By Marion Grogan

A real taste of Spring using the first rhubarb of the year.

Preparation time 15 minutes *Cooking time* 40 minutes
Equipment Two 1lb loaf tins, lightly greased *Makes* 20 slices

Ingredients

225ml/8fl oz buttermilk
1 tablespoon lemon juice
1 teaspoon vanilla extract
225g/8oz dark brown sugar
150ml/¼ pint vegetable oil
1 egg

300g/11oz plain flour
1 teaspoon salt
1 teaspoon bread soda
175g/6oz chopped rhubarb
75g/3oz chopped walnuts

Topping:
4 tablespoons dark brown sugar
½ teaspoon ground cinnamon
1 tablespoon butter, melted

Method

1. Preheat the oven to 160C/325F/Gas mark 3.

2. In a small bowl, stir together the buttermilk, lemon juice and vanilla. Let stand for 10 minutes.

3. In a separate large bowl, mix together the brown sugar, oil and egg.

4. Combine the flour, salt and bread soda, and stir into the sugar mixture alternatively with the milk mixture until all three are just combined.

5. Fold in the rhubarb and nuts.

6. Pour the batter into the prepared loaf tins.

7. In a small bowl combine the brown sugar, cinnamon and butter.

8. Sprinkle this mixture over the unbaked loaves.

9. Bake in a preheated oven for 40-45 minutes, until a skewer inserted into the centre of the loaf comes out clean.

Traditional Fruit Cake

By Betty Hooks

Everyone loves traditional fruit cake. Leaving the fruit to soak overnight makes it deliciously moist and once you've done that the rest of this recipe only takes minutes to prepare.

Preparation time 10 minutes, plus 6 hours or overnight *Cooking time* 50-55 minutes
Equipment Loaf tin *Makes* 15 slices

Ingredients

350g/12oz mixed fruit
300ml/½ pint tea

225g/8oz self-raising flour
½ teaspoon of bread soda

1 large egg, beaten

Method

1. Combine the tea and fruit and soak for 6 hours or overnight.

2. Next day, preheat the oven to 180C/350F/Gas mark 4.

3. Sieve the flour and bread soda together and add it to the fruit, mixing well.

4. Stir in the beaten egg.

5. Pour the mixture into the loaf tin and bake for 50-55 minutes until golden brown.

6. Delicious served warm with a thick layer of butter.

Christmas Pudding

By Nelly (Ellen) Coffey

This is Nelly's well-loved family recipe given to us by her granddaughter, Paula. These puddings can be made ahead up to two months before eating.

Preparation time 30 minutes *Cooking time* Simmer for 6 hrs
Equipment Greaseproof paper and tinfoil, two pudding bowls
Makes A large 1 litre/2 pint & a smaller 250ml/½ pint pudding

Ingredients

250g/8oz self-raising flour
250g/8oz breadcrumbs
250g/8oz dark brown sugar
350g/12oz raisins
350g/12oz sultanas
100g/4oz candied peel
2 teaspoons cinnamon

2 teaspoons nutmeg
1 large cooking apple, grated
Rind and juice of 1 large lemon
250g/8oz butter
2 large eggs
2 tablespoons rum
300ml/½ pint beer or stout

Method

1. Mix all the dry ingredients together in a large mixing bowl.

2. Add the lemon rind and juice and the grated cooking apple.

3. Melt the butter slightly and add it to the mixture along with the eggs, rum, and beer/stout.

4. Grease the two pudding bowls with butter and pour the mixture in up to three-quarters full.

5. Cover the bowls with greaseproof paper, then tinfoil, and tie around the rim with string.

6. For each pudding, place a saucer upside-down on the bottom of a saucepan and put the pudding on top. Fill the saucepan up to one-third with boiling water.

7. Allow to return to the boil, then simmer the puddings for 5-6 hours, replenishing with boiling water when necessary.

8. When cooked, allow to cool, then re-cover with clean greaseproof paper and store in a cool, dry place.

9. On Christmas day, re-cover with greased greaseproof paper and foil and boil for 2-3 hours.

Nelly, or Ellen as she was christened, was always a great cook, everyone knew this, and friends and neighbours would come in to the house on a Sunday morning to enjoy her homemade food. Ellen's husband Mick especially loved her recipes. He was a fine athlete, and boxed with the famous Garda Lugs Brannigan, known for his down-to earth and 'real' approach to dealing with troublemakers. Ellen, on the other hand, likes a different kind of reality, one that favours escapism. She loves reading and watching television. Listening to music, especially the Three Tenors and Phil Coulter, is a special kind of pleasure for her.

In later life, Ellen said, 'I became the Virgin Granny, because I was adopted, and my daughter was adopted too.' It was at the age of eight years old that Ellen was adopted by her new family in Crumlin. She went on to recreate that happy experience in her own life when she was blessed with her beautiful daughter, Paula through adoption. Paula was her devoted carer until she came to the Extended Care Unit in Our Lady's Hospice & Care Services, and she remained Ellen's most precious friend.

Name:

By:

Preparation time   *Cooking time*
Equipment
Serves

Ingredients

Method

Notes

Name:

By:

Preparation time *Cooking time*
Equipment
Serves

Ingredients

Method

Notes

Name:

By:

Preparation time · · · · · Cooking time
Equipment
Serves

Ingredients

Notes

Method

Name:

By:

Preparation time   *Cooking time*
Equipment
Serves

Ingredients

Method

Notes

Name:

By:

Preparation time   *Cooking time*
Equipment
Serves

Ingredients

Method

Notes

Conversions

Weight

1oz/25g	8oz/225g	15 oz/425g	2lb 3oz/1kg
2oz/50g	9oz/250g	16 oz/1Lb/450g	1lb ¾/800g
3oz/75g	10oz/275g	1lb 2oz/18oz/500g	1lb 14oz/850g
4oz/110g	11oz/300g	1lb 3oz/550g	2lb/900g
5oz/150g	12oz/350g	1lb 5oz/600g	
6oz/175g	13 oz/375g	1lb 6oz/625g	
7oz/200g	14oz/400g	1lb 8oz/700g	

Temperature

90°C/185°F/Gas mark ¼	130°C/260°F/Gas mark ½	170°C/325°F/Gas mark 3	220°C/425°F/Gas mark 7
100°C/200°F/Gas mark ¼	140°C/275°F/Gas mark 1	180°C/350°F/Gas mark 4	230°C/450°F/Gas mark 8
110°C/230/Gas mark ¼	150°C/300°F/Gas mark 2	190°C/375°F/Gas mark 5	240°C/475°F/Gas mark 9
120°C/250°F/Gas mark ½	160°C/325°F/Gas mark 3	200°C/400°F/Gas mark 6	

Liquid

2fl oz/50ml	8fl oz/225ml	14fl oz/400ml	20fl oz/1 pint/600ml
3fl oz/75ml	9fl oz/275ml	15fl oz/425ml	30fl oz/1 ½ pints/850ml
4 fl oz/125ml	10fl oz/300ml	16fl oz/475ml	2 pints/1 litre
5fl oz/150ml	11fl oz/325ml	17fl oz/500ml	
6fl oz/175ml	12fl oz/350ml	18fl oz/500ml	
7fl oz/200ml	13fl oz/375ml	19fl oz/550ml	

Important: This conversion table has been created for the purpose of this book and the recipes included within. It is not a universal guide and users should be aware that discrepancies and variations between measurements, temperatures and volumes may exist for the purpose of suiting a particular recipe and should be followed with care.

In many cases conversions in recipes may have been rounded up or down in one or more of the offered formats for ease of use. Some of the recipes supplied have slightly different conversions shown and in these cases we have used the contributor's measurements and conversions in each recipe in order to ensure the recipe is true to their intent.